Only Say

Praise for John Davies' earlier

Be Born in Us Today: The Message of the Incarnation

'These meditations come as a refreshing surprise'

Archbishop Rowan Williams

'assists readers to see with new eyes and make connections between the biblical accounts of the birth of Christ and the world experienced today'

Anglican Encounter

'disturbingly cutting-edge'

Expository Times

The Crisis of the Cross

'Piercing insight(s) . . . are typical of the perceptiveness and literary elegance of a publication deserving a long shelf life'

Church Times

'powerful and challenging'

Catholic Herald

'skilfully combines good scholarship with a deeply perceptive understanding'

Transmission

God at Work: Creation Then and Now

'. . . deceptively easy to read, but the contents are profound'

The Franciscan

'the book is littered with wonderful touches'

Bishop John Saxbee

'. . . reflective and challenging . . . a book that combines wisdom with delight'

Esther de Waal

John D. Davies was Bishop of Shrewsbury from 1987 to 1994. Previously, he spent many years in rural parish and city university ministry in South Africa, Wales and England. He is a former principal of the College of the Ascension in Birmingham and a Residentiary Canon of St Asaph Cathedral.

The author of numerous books and Bible study guides, he is now retired and lives near Llangollen, North Wales. With his wife, Shirley, he is an associate of the Iona Community.

He is the author of *The Crisis of the Cross*, *Be Born in Us Today* and *God at Work*, also published by the Canterbury Press.

Only Say the Word

Interactive Bible Studies on Healing and Salvation

John Davies

with diagrams by
Clive Edwards

CANTERBURY
PRESS
Norwich

To the second-hand camel-dealer (see Chapter 18), and all
the other people who have worked with us on these stories
over many years.

Text © John Davies 2002
Diagrams © Clive Edwards 2002

First published in 2002 by the Canterbury Press Norwich
(a publishing imprint of Hymns Ancient & Modern Limited,
a registered charity)
St Mary's Works, St Mary's Plain,
Norwich, Norfolk, NR3 3BH

www.scm-canterburypress.co.uk

British Library Cataloguing in Publication data

A catalogue record for this book is available
from the British Library

Bible passages are quoted from *The Dramatised Bible*
published by The Bible Society

1-85311-498-7

Typeset by Regent Typesetting, London
Printed in Great Britain by
Bookmarque, Croydon, Surrey

Contents

Foreword

by Shirley Davies

This book is about salvation, on the one hand, and is a method of Bible study, on the other hand. It could be described as a 'do-it-yourself' book, in which we search for what salvation means for us today.

For me, salvation comes about mainly through incarnation, God interfering and intervening in the world and particularly in the Church. The themes of this book are about looking at the Bible stories we have inherited, and working out what salvation means in that context. There are many astute insights and challenges offered to us by way of interpreting the various stories and events. I hope what John has to offer you will prove helpful in your journey of discovering what it means to be a Christian in the twenty-first century. We face situations for which there are no records in the Bible, for example, nuclear power, weapons of mass destruction, and the power of advertisements and the media generally.

The process that is recommended in this book is something I have come to value over many years. This is mainly because this method keeps the Bible story alive in the memory, simply through being involved with the characters. John and I have worked with many hundreds of people over the years with this method and they have brought many new insights into biblical study. We have been both challenged and changed by people who take their Christian responsibility seriously.

But I want to appeal to the reader on another issue. The method also represents John and me working together – the trained and the untrained. I have not studied theology academically; I have no qualifications for being a 'teacher' other than being a Christian. It is an ideal method for trained and untrained to work together. Most church congregations have within them a vast amount of what I call *corporate memory*, an accumulated wealth of information collected as a result of listening week by week, year by year, to the reading of the Bible. This 'memory bank' should be enabled and encouraged. The trained and the untrained must come together to work out the theological basis for our place in the world. It is not a question of one being more important than the other, one being more educated than the other. Each must discover what the other holds in the mind of God. This method is close to the style of Jesus: a kind of apprenticeship method, learning on the job. The disciples of Jesus then and the disciples of Jesus now are to face and work through the issues that present themselves today. What a challenge!

Jesus gave us a model of salvation by the way he treated people. He saw beyond the problems that people presented; he saw the potential of each person. We need to take this model on board as we meet and encounter each other. Theology for me is a verb, a *doing* word. I do not mean being a doer in terms of action only, I mean doing in terms of searching and working out. This book gives us plenty of opportunity to do just that.

Use the corporate memory, which is stored in everyone, to 'do' Bible study and work out together what salvation means for each person and community today. I hope that you will feel challenged and empowered both by the method and the message of this book.

Shirley Davies
Gobowen
April 2002

Author's Note

One of the original inspirations for this book was the work we did with Dr John Vincent at the Urban Theology Unit, Sheffield. Some years ago, John Vincent and I produced a book of studies on Mark's Gospel entitled *Mark at Work*. This has been out of print for a long time now. I am very grateful to him for his generous encouragement in the writing of the present book; at many points, as indicated in the Notes, it depends on our previous publication. I hope that, in a small way, it may encourage John and his colleagues as they continue in their pioneering work of journeying.

As Shirley, my wife, has emphasized in her Foreword, this book represents many occasions when she and I have been able to collaborate in all sorts of events and programmes. Without question, these have been the most valuable educational experiences of my life in the last 25 years. We write this now, with a sense that we owe it to the many people who have worked with us over these years, in small groups and larger conferences: on Iona, in Wales, England and in various places outside the UK. Occasionally, in the following pages, I write in the first-person singular, usually to give an example of how one can link one's own experience to some element in the Bible story. But otherwise, this book is cast in the form of 'we', and this 'we' refers to Shirley and me together. Often, we have been able to offer a programme as a double-act. This collaboration between two very dissimilar people has been one of the features that has caused most comment from people whom we have worked with. In many ways, this book is a double-act too. It would not have its present character if it were not for Shirley's initiatives and criticisms.

One of the best reactions to our work came at the end of a big diocesan clergy conference. Some of the members were approaching us with invitations such as, 'Please come and do this sort of thing for us in our parish'. The Bishop jumped in quite fiercely and told them, 'You have seen how this sort of approach works; now go and do it yourself.' Amen to that.

John D. Davies
Gobowen
Festival of St Mark, 2002

Part One
Approaches

1

Jesus the Story-Maker

This is a book about stories. So here is a story to begin with.

A novice monk was given the job of assisting a preacher at a beach mission. With the help of some students, he was required to go round the deckchairs, and gather people to form a congregation. Then he had to stand around in his cassock during the sermon, and catch people to talk to afterwards. To his relief, he saw a notice saying, 'Bathing Costumes for Hire'. He slipped quietly away and hired one – a 1950s model, black, with shoulder straps. He got into it, and rejoined the crowd. A few minutes later, one of the students, not recognizing him without his cassock and glasses, pursued him.

'Have you been saved?' she tenderly enquired.

'Saved?' he said. 'I've not been in yet.'

The story is told by our friend Eric James.[1] The novice monk was Fr Gerard, CR, whom I knew as Geoffrey Beaumont, my College Chaplain when I was a student. Later, he joined our team of university chaplains in South Africa, when his Community set up a house in Stellenbosch. The story is completely in character. Geoffrey was one of the redeeming features of Cambridge for me. I had come there from the RAF. In its educational method and in its lack of a practical sense of purpose, the university was something of a comedown. When I was being trained to maintain and repair aircraft, our instructors were always telling us, 'If you don't do that job better, someone's going to get killed.' (This, of course, was rather disregarding the

fact that if we repaired a bomber properly, a whole lot of
other people were likely to get killed – but that's another
problem.) By contrast, the main purpose of our studies at
university seemed to be to pass examinations – a compara-
tively uninspiring incentive. Geoffrey was not only a brilliant
story-teller; he was a story in himself. He was one of those
people who make religion tolerable.

I finished theological studies with a well-developed skill
in writing doctrinal essays on such subjects as 'Salvation',
for the purpose of passing examinations. Then I went to a
very practical and innovative parish to work as a curate
(where Shirley and I met and married). Like many new
ministers, I quickly found that there was little market for
such essays, and that my carefully acquired skills were not
much in demand. The people of our parish were certainly
not theological illiterates – they engaged with questions
about the mission of God's people in the world with a commitment and awareness such as I have never met elsewhere.[2]
But they didn't thrive on doctrinal theory; they were story-
tellers. They were constantly swapping anecdotes across
garden fences, in pubs, in church meetings. So I started to
preach from stories and cartoons in scurrilous magazines. I
came to realize that the Christian gospel is primarily a
story, and that the Gospel narratives are a better point of
entry than the writings of St Paul. Even the Epistles are
events in history; they make best sense when they are
seen as contributions to ongoing arguments and explorations.

This is all very obvious and commonplace now. When
The Dramatised Bible appeared, it demonstrated that most
of the Bible is narrative. Its sheer size – it's more like a
missile than a book – is evidence that God communicates
with us through events; he has made most of us to be story-
tellers rather than theory-builders. We may have occasional
doubts about its translation, but I tell parish clergy that
they need to be able to give a good excuse for *not* using *The*

Dramatised Bible for the routine Gospel readings in the liturgy.

After about 30 years of trying to teach and preach about the Gospels, among African peasants, and university students in South Africa and Britain, I gradually came to realize that we don't need to expound these stories. All we need to do is to give people some leading questions, so that they can work at the stories with their own imagination, and see the events from the points of view of the various characters in the stories. This book represents some of the discoveries made by many groups of people, in local churches, conferences and study-groups, where Shirley and I have been invited to participate. I may be the individual author; but the book is really formed by the faith and commitment of communities. In this sense, it is similar to the Gospels themselves; they are the product of individual writers, but they are brought into existence by the commitment, the faith, the discoveries, the struggles and the memories, of various communities of Christian disciples.

In this book, we look at some of the stories in the Gospels of Matthew, Mark and Luke, and we examine virtually every occasion where the Evangelist uses the word 'save' or 'salvation'.[3] The central figure in each case is Jesus. But there are various other characters, and in the groupwork we ask members, in small teams, to identify with these characters. If we read them in this dramatic way, all sorts of features start to emerge, which are not necessarily so clear if we just read the stories as monologues.

The little story about Geoffrey Beaumont is a story concerning 'being saved' – salvation. All the stories in this book are, in one way or another, about salvation. In many of them, the actual word for 'save' appears. Where it does not, the story is still a story about Jesus; and 'Jesus' in Hebrew is virtually the same as 'Saviour'; in these other stories, there is still a saving kind of experience. Some sort of miracle or change or new opportunity is taking place. One of the discoveries that we make when we work on these stories in small groups is that there is always some surprise, some tension or some significant change. Often there is a conflict of interest; different groups of people have different agendas, different irons in the fire. The friends of the paralytic are at odds with the crowd in the house; the scribes have another set of priorities. When we have small teams of people looking at these characters from their different points of view, the processes and costs of 'salvation' start to jump into focus.

Modern scholars like to put these stories into categories, and one such category is 'miracle-story'. This is a sort of classification that can make good sense in some circumstances, just as the difference between mineral and vegetable is important in some circumstances. Salt and pepper are very different things in a laboratory or greenhouse; they sit together happily in the kitchen or on the sideboard. In the theological library, perhaps, the classification into 'miracle-stories', 'pronouncement-stories', and so on, can be interesting, but for people who are at the cutting-edge of the Christian movement, who are trying to be disciples in the world, the difference between stories that are 'miracle-stories' and those that are not is not particularly important. It is a distinction that clearly did not matter much to Matthew, Mark and Luke. They put their stories together regardless of this kind of category; for them, they were all stories about salvation. Zacchaeus's sudden commitment to justice, or the opening up of the mind of the lawyer, was no less remarkable than the healing of a paralytic or the cleansing of a leper.

Another feature of these stories is that so many of them involve journeys and movement. Many of them become much clearer when we act out the journeys on the floor, or work out the movements on diagrams. This is true, for instance, in the story of the ten lepers, or the story of Jairus and the woman with the haemorrhage.

In most of the stories, there is a 'third party' – someone

other than Jesus and the person who is being attended to by him. It may be the Disciples, or the crowd, or someone, like the Pharisee Simon, who is involved in the event. They get in the way, or they comment, or they help, or they observe, or they are affected by the outcome. Their reactions are important in the working-out of the significance of the event. The Disciples are there as part of their training. They observe what happens when God is at work in the world. They are brought together for teaching; they are sent off to practise what they have learned; they return for more teaching. It was not modern technological education that invented the sandwich course: it was Jesus of Nazareth.

When people get into the role of Jesus, they realize that many of the things that happen surprise him. Sometimes, this is made explicit by the Evangelist – in the story of the Canaanite woman, for instance, or that of the centurion's boy. Jesus is not in control all the time; he does not know exactly who is going to do what. He learns as he goes along. Because he is constantly learning, he has the authority to teach.

Further, as a story proceeds, there is often a question for Jesus of what course of action to take. There are several options, and it can be helpful to look at these and see what are the implications of his decision. How far does he allow himself to be interrupted? How far does he put his reputation at risk? What does he stand to gain and to lose if he follows certain lines of action? How does he sort out the conflicting claims on his time and attention – in, for instance, the Jairus/woman story? These are not just matters of theoretical speculation. One of the guiding principles of this sort of study is that we, the readers or receivers, are the Body of Christ. In us, God is seeking to continue the Christ-work and the Christ-message. If we see what happens to Jesus, God Incarnate, we can derive guidelines for our own programme and our own purposes, as disciples. If we are truly the Body of Christ, very probably we shall find ourselves being pulled around in different directions, as we are on the receiving end of conflicting interests. We need not be surprised if we run into the same sort of hassles that pulled Jesus around.

The Evangelist in question – Matthew, Mark or Luke – is part of the story. If it were not for him, and the people for whom he wrote, there would be no story. As we read the page, we depend on the effect that the story had on the Evangelist and the Church for which he wrote. The story is evidence, evidence of the faith of the Evangelist and the fact that he thought that the story was worth recording – bearing in mind that the great majority of things that Jesus did and said are irretrievably lost (John 21:25). Why did the Evangelist record this story in the way he did? Why, for instance, do the Evangelists record the Jairus/woman story as a single complex narrative, rather than tell it as two distinct events, as some subsequent editors have preferred to do? The Evangelist's purpose, and the needs of the Church for which he wrote, are part of the material presented to us on the page. So it is always worthwhile to include the story-teller as one of the roles in the exploration.

And we ourselves are part of the story. We do not come to it cold. We come with centuries of interpretation and of Christian piety behind us. Sometimes, this may obstruct the meaning; it may blunt the cutting-edge of the story, or of Jesus' words, by over-familiarity, or by being bent to suit the conventions or authority-systems of our time. But we also bring our own valuable experiences of being human in our world. We have our own experiences of hope and disappointment, of delay and debt and disability; we make connections; we find ourselves on the page that we are reading.

In most of these stories, Jesus is clearly acting as Saviour. He restores the intentions of the Creator. He sets people free. He defies the powers that destroy people's wholeness;

he encourages defiance in others. He does not send people away, telling them to accept their disabilities as the will of God. True, this is not effortless magic; there are costs and delays and controversies. But he is there in power, and the gospel is his success. And then there is the 'other half' of the story, represented in this book by Chapter 19. He saved others; himself he cannot save. And this 'failure' is not only on Good Friday. When we have this clue to his work, we see that it is woven into the fabric of his ministry from the beginning. He does not come dispensing gifts like Father Christmas does. He comes sharing human disaster, weakness and loss. Further, this is part of the calling that he invites his disciples to share. Unless we take this side of the story seriously, we shall miss out a major part of what 'salvation' is about; and we shall betray the interests of many of our colleagues in Christian discipleship who are themselves suffering from deprivations for which there are at present no cures. There is something deeply wrong with our understanding of the gospel if its effect is to make such people feel that they are second-class or marginal, that they represent failure or that they are signs of God's rejection. Our culture seems to be well supplied with people who are in business to make a profit out of other people's disabilities. Each phase of unemployment generates a fresh batch of advisors and consultants and trainers, whose contribution often leaves the unemployed people feeling more angry and disappointed than before. Let the Church beware of trying to be strong and active, to demean those who happen to be weak and helpless.[4]

Certainly, the Church, in its response to Jesus, is called to fight and to rebel against the cruelties and injustices that afflict us. It does have a message of good news for the poor. But Jesus is also the one who accepts limitations and is creative within them. He accepts human judgement and condemnation, because he saves us from within our situation, not as a mechanism from outside. The faith that fights needs to be partnered by the faith that accepts. In practice, there seem to be at least three proper kinds of further response. It may be best to suggest these here, rather than try to spell them out in each separate piece of narrative.

First, the ministry of Jesus is to integrate. We shall be seeing some of the implications of Paul's great Easter statement, 'there is no longer Greek and Jew, circumcised and uncircumcised, barbarian, Scythian, slave and free' (Colossians 3:11); we must extend this into, 'no longer disabled and non-disabled, no longer productive and unproductive'. This was never a simple and non-controversial message, and still raises plenty of objections. But we insist that in Christ we belong with each other; all are relatively abled, relatively dis-abled, in a Church that is a patients' co-operative. We need to check how far this is really true, in local situations. We need to ask how far the more dis-abled people feel that they really belong.

Secondly, Christians have been faithful to the gospel when, in all sorts of places and circumstances, they have set up schemes and institutions to serve sick people, lepers, deaf people, blind people. The Gospel stories have inspired the followers of Jesus with a belief that whatever can be done should be done. So, for instance, schools for deaf people may not have provided instant hearing for their children; but they have enabled communication. And it does seem to be a particularly Christian initiative that gets this sort of enterprise into existence.

But, thirdly, this is not just the fortunate working for the unfortunate. It means recognizing, disclosing and affirming the human creativity and value of the apparently dis-abled or abnormal person. The ministry of Jesus was consistently affirming the value of people for whom society gave little value. This was the sign of the presence of God, more than any subsequent physical change. The dis-ability can become a gift, not only to the sufferer but also to the community as a whole. So Deaf people can affirm their rights and values and culture as Deaf people, and not merely as failed-hearing people. They develop a language that is natural and right for them, and hearing people need to respect this creativity and not coerce them into assimilation into hearing culture. Homosexual people are not adjusted to express physical love according to the norms of heterosexual people – they develop a language and style of physical love which is natural and right for them; this again is their creativity, in spite of the grudging attitude of the official Church.

It is very often the structures and conventions of the majority world that tell 'disabled' people they are disabled. A wheelchair-user is awarded an MBE for her 'Services to the Disabled' – and at the Investiture she has to be given her award in a corridor because there is no access for her in the main reception room. Should not the other recipients have demanded to be given their Honours in the corridor also? The use of the negative term 'disabled' sounds uncomfortably close to the old South African term 'non-European' – defining people in terms of what they are not. The way that 'dis-abled' people are treated would not be tolerated if it were a matter of race or gender.

At this point, it is clear that the two ways of faith belong together. Defiance and acceptance belong together in the calling of Jesus.

2

Meanings of 'Salvation'

In the course of these stories from the Gospels, we meet great words such as 'save', 'salvation' and 'faith'. We can detach ourselves from all the complexities that theologians have loaded onto these words over the centuries, and ask, 'What actually do these words mean in this particular context?' What is being referred to when Jesus commends the faith of the woman at Simon's house, or the tenth leper, or the friends of the paralytic? What has happened for Jesus to speak of the 'salvation' of Zacchaeus or of the woman with the haemorrhage or the tenth leper? It would, perhaps, be possible to make a coherent generalization from all these instances, and attempt an inclusive definition. But this is not what the text invites us to do. We come at each instance in its own particular character. We will not derive a complete definition from any one instance; but we collect a series of windows into the total meaning, and this will help us to recognize 'salvation' when it happens in our own experience.

A great theme such as 'salvation' is like a sculpture. No one person can see the whole of it; we move around it, catching different angles and different views. There is a recognizable coherence – a sculpture of a woman and man embracing is different from a model of the Forth Bridge. But for one person it will be directed to the right, and to another it will be directed to the left. Each viewer will have a different angle on it. Each separate story also is like a sculpture; it can be seen from different points of view, and no one is going to be able to say that they can see the whole of it at once. It is not a thing-in-itself; it depends on being seen. The sculptor Naum Gabo wrote:[1]

> The artist makes the work: the viewer makes it art. A work of art, restricted to what the artist has put into it, is only part of itself. It attains full status only with what people and time make of it.

Each reader of one of these stories contributes to its meaning by bringing a personal history. One will have a particular experience of paralysis; another will be interested in providing transport. A group member who has been engaged with the story from the point of view of Jairus will tell it very differently from one who has got into the experience of the woman with the haemorrhage.

In the stories themselves, different people need salvation in different ways. The woman with the haemorrhage, for instance, is terribly scared of being visible, of coming out into the open, of losing her anonymity in the general mass of people. In a word, she is afraid of isolation. She has to be enabled to 'come out', to stand on her own. Her salvation is, at least in part, this willingness to overcome this fear. Jesus gives her the confidence to be distinctive, to own her own story. Zacchaeus, by contrast, has shaped his life on a project to put himself at a distance from the general mass of people. His hope is to escape from the poverty around him; so, he has created a detached nest for himself. He is afraid of merely being absorbed into the common lot of humanity. He has to be enabled to 'come down', to join the common people, to live in terms of solidarity with the poor rather than isolation from the poor. Jesus gives him this confidence, so that he surrenders the isolating wealth that he has accumulated. For him, this is 'salvation'. So, two very different experiences, but one enabler of the salvation.

At this point, we can see in Jesus a sign of the eternal

nature of God as Trinity. God is not just a solitary point of absolute power, high up in the heavens, but an eternal community, three persons. That community holds us in security; we can risk taking the kind of action that may isolate us, because the principle of community is guaranteed in the eternal nature of God. But God also is diversity, three persons who are eternally distinct. We do not have to insist on our separateness or detach ourselves from solidarity, because the principle of personal distinctiveness is guaranteed in the eternal nature of God. Salvation for the woman and salvation for Zacchaeus are significantly different, but both come into the fellowship of the saved.

So this way of coming at the scripture must depend on freedom to discover. There is no uniform, definitive interpretation of these stories. The leader of the study must not give the impression that she or he knows it all in advance, and that the group members just have to catch up. The leader will always be a learner. Each of these stories is like a parable: it is not given to make a single, definite point, but rather to enable members to explore their world and their faith, to take responsibility for their own understanding. Occasionally the leader may have to help to clarify facts, for example, the meaning of certain words – like Zacchaeus's 'sycamore tree' – or the historical background. But rarely will the leader need to say that someone's understanding of a story is actually wrong. Often it may be incomplete; often it may be so encrusted with traditional piety that a bit of gentle chisel-work may be needed. Usually there will be sufficient variety within the group for this to happen without the leader having to intervene. Everyone's insight is needed.

So, a story in the Gospels, like a work of art, depends on those who receive it. It is a story of salvation; and that means that it gives space to those who read and receive, to grow, to be and to discover.

Can we make any generalizations about the meaning of great words such as 'salvation' and 'faith'? If we put the stories together, we can say that 'faith' very often involves some sort of defiance of norms and expectations and regulations; and 'salvation' is often something for which the saved person, and not the 'Saviour', takes responsibility. One of the recurring comments of Jesus is, 'Your faith has saved you'. He does not demand that anyone should give him credit for their salvation. On the contrary, he avoids making people dependent on himself. He meets people who have little self-esteem and are used to being treated as dependent or as claimants or as disabled or as rubbish, and he affirms that it is something from inside themselves that has made the difference. Is Jesus then redundant? No; he creates the environment in which this sort of discovery can be made. And that, again, is the role of the Church, as the Body of Christ. Our Bible study will have served one of its primary purposes if it has the effect of encouraging people to claim their own ability to live and move and make judgements, rather than be dependent on systems and structures for which they have not themselves taken some responsibility.

But there seem to be problems with Jesus' words, 'Your faith has saved you'. This is a point at which those who have some knowledge of Greek have a responsibility for sharing their concerns with their fellow-disciples. Many of the standard translations into English insist on expressing Jesus' words as 'Your faith has made you well' (this is the translation given at various places in *The Dramatised Bible*, but I have amended it to 'saved' in this book). But being 'saved' is not the same as merely 'getting well'. We can see from Luke's careful use of verbs in the story of the healing of the Ten Lepers that 'curing', 'healing' and 'saving' are three quite distinct experiences (see Chapter 14 below). The Jerusalem Bible's version makes this clear. 'Getting well' means going back to a previous state of health or fitness; 'being saved' means going on into some new relationship to the Creator, some new confidence within the world. In the case of the woman in Simon's house (see Chapter 11 below), the woman has not been, in any ordinary sense of the word, 'ill'; so the translators cannot take refuge in such a phrase as 'getting well'. They give us the plain meaning of the word 'save'. But elsewhere, why, on the whole, do our translators avoid this? Is it because they want to reserve the use of the word 'save' exclusively to the direct, unilateral, supernatural and eternal action of God? And is that, in turn, because we want to keep a monopoly of 'salvation' to the organized Church, which knows about these things and carries the responsibility for administering the Word and the Sacraments to the faithful?

Many examples in history, from popular dissatisfaction with mediaeval Catholicism to popular rejection of Marxist Communism, show that if an organization, however benign, claims to have a monopoly of the means of grace, it will be met by the demands of personal faith or responsibility. *Sola gratia* will be replaced by *sola fide*. To work on these stories with small groups of people is to discover faith, in places where the organized life of the Church often lets it lie concealed. In our own small way, we see where it can still be true to say, 'Your faith has saved you'.

Reflecting on my time as Principal of a missionary training college, I can identify the most common misunderstanding about the meaning of 'salvation' in modern Christian circles, namely that it means deliverance from the world of daily experience into some distant 'heaven'. It is deliverance from a world of power and struggle and sex and money. It is, in effect, deliverance from the Creation; the Saviour saves us from the work of the Creator. But in the Hebrew Scriptures, and in the ministry of Jesus, 'salvation' was something happening in this present world. For Hebrew-thinking people of New Testament times, the words 'save' and 'salvation' had the primary meaning of being *given space*. The Hebrews had been an oppressed people, trapped in slavery, without a voice, with no access to the wealth created by their labour, and with no land to call their own.

'Salvation' was what happened in Exodus. It was itself the work of the Creator. Negatively, they were delivered from slavery. Positively, they were provided with open space, the Promised Land, an area for which they could take responsibility. In their songs celebrating deliverance, they praised God, who had 'set their feet in a broad space' (Psalms 18:19; 31:8). Moses faced Pharaoh with God's demand, 'Let my people go'. The people travelled to find their home – 'my home is over Jordan'. Enslaved people down the centuries pick up this double meaning of salvation. They celebrate it and sing it. They know it as a reality to be found in this world. For the black slaves moving along 'the underground railroad' in the USA, 'Jordan' was not only the boundary of death, it was also the Ohio, the river dividing the slave-states from the free. They knew the biblical meaning of 'salvation'.

Salvation, as experienced in the Gospel stories about Jesus, has these two meanings. It is deliverance from oppression of various kinds. It is also the entry into home, a free space. It celebrates the glory and goodness of the Creator's intention. Sometimes, this is restoration. The paralytic and the Gerasene and the daughter of Jairus are restored to their homes. They belong again to their communities. But not every community is a place of salvation. A community can be a trap, a conspiracy of exclusiveness, of rejection, of dependence on special qualifications. It can be something to be saved from. So there are some for whom salvation is entry into a completely new community. The tenth leper joins a fellowship of thanksgiving; Bartimaeus follows 'in the way'. The Canaanite woman and the centurion become the pioneers of a new opportunity of access for Gentiles. In the Temple, Jesus makes space for various people who had been excluded. So the Saviour is not someone who takes you out of one trap and then locks you into another. He is one who enables your freedom and responsibility.

Behind all this, there is the metaphor and model of the land. At the heart of the Law of Moses was the principle of Sabbath and of Jubilee, the guarantee that all the people had a right to the land and of access to it. Jesus, as the bringer of salvation, restores to people their place within the community, their rights of access to the common inheritance. The people's rights in the land had been severely weakened by political developments, by the time of Jesus. Roman colonization had brought an occupying army, with all sorts of hangers-on and exploiters. Land-tenure itself had got into the hands of large-scale estates, owned by absentee landlords and managed by rapacious underlings. All this can be read from the parables of Jesus. An informative account of the socio-economic situation of the land of Palestine could be derived from his teaching.

But of even greater significance for Jesus was the way that people's confidence in God and in themselves had been weakened by the religious systems of the day, based on the application of the purity laws of the Scriptures. As the Basque philosopher Unamuno pointed out, tradition can be like a skeleton, hidden inside the body, giving it strength, or it can be an external shell, holding life in.[2] In Jesus' time, religion, especially the gracious and liberating laws of the Sabbath, had become a shell. In the absence of a legitimate political outlet, people had turned their energies into institutional religion – something that is only too easy to recognize in our own world. Time and again, Jesus found that people's understanding of God was acting as a fence to keep other people out. He met the victims of this attitude, people who were not qualified, who were excluded from the community of holiness, who were 'sinners', 'unclean', 'dis-abled'. He treated them as responsible and acceptable people, and so he dis-abled the purity system itself. He claimed that all foods were clean; he was willing to be touched and contaminated. He showed that the whole edifice of purity and religious qualifications was obsolete.

This would have all sorts of implications for the economy. The sacrificial system of the Temple depended on people's sense of the need for purification and forgiveness. The distinction between clean and unclean food had effects on the meat industry and the exchange of goods between Jew and Gentile. We run into this sort of issue in almost every one of these stories of salvation. More than any other single matter, salvation is deliverance from the rules of purity and of moral qualifications. Surely, it is not an exaggeration to say that if the Anglican Church, in recent years, had taken the Gospel stories of Jesus as its guidelines, rather than the logic of theoretical principles, it would never have got itself into such a mess as it has about the issues of the place of women in ministry and the status of homosexual people.

When I was about halfway through writing this book, a friend commended to me the Church of England Doctrinal Commission's report 'The Mystery of Salvation'.[3] I have been glad to see this. It provides an excellent review of the understandings of 'salvation' that have been developed down the centuries. But I found myself wondering why it felt so distant from my own world and why it engaged my commitment so little. Then I realized that not only did it pay very little attention to the stories of Jesus, but also that it contained hardly any stories about anyone at all – except, most significantly, in the one area where it was exploring new ground, namely in its engaging with non-Christian faiths. The writers of this report are people of great distinction, and some of them we are glad to know as friends. But their feet seem to be more in the university library than on the streets where Jesus was. This present book is not in the same league and will not serve the same purpose. But it does represent a kind of research done not through books but by enabling people to explore and express their experiences. And that is a necessary part of any engaging with the Scriptures.

There was a time when the Bible was seen to be the

exclusive preserve of the clergy, and the laity were protected from exposure to it. More recently, it has become the domain of academic experts. Our intention is to contribute to the re-claiming of the Bible as the possession of the *whole* people of God; not just as an object of dispassionate study and investigation but also as a resource for struggle, commitment and discipleship.

3

The Second Christians

We are in the age of the second Christians. The first Christians were the people who were affected by Jesus directly, and who recognized something of the truth about him. A mixed group they were. For instance, there was a non-commissioned officer of a colonial army of occupation, whose duties included the supervision of crucifixions. This centurion was the first person to recognize the crucified Son of God (Mark 15:39). In this sense, he was one of the first Christians. Then there was the first person to recognize the risen Christ, a person who, on account of being female, would not be accepted as a credible witness in a contemporary court of law: Mary Magdalene, also one of the first Christians (Mark 16:1; John 20:1–18). Then there were the people whom Jesus himself called, an unpromising collection of men with no great education or social prestige, who were consistent only in misunderstanding and getting in the way (e.g. Mark 1:16–20; 9:33–35; 10:13–14). The disciples also were the first Christians. On the evidence given by this tiny handful of improbable people, countless millions of us have been convinced about the meaning of Jesus.

Soon, another group of Christians came into being – the second Christians. They were convinced by the message brought by the first Christians. They committed themselves to the new Kingdom, which Jesus had announced, but they heard of this Kingdom through the message of the first Christians, not directly from Jesus himself. In other ways, moreover, their situation was different. Most of the second Christians were not living in Jerusalem or Galilee; their problems did not centre around the complaints of Jewish temple-officials and local nationalists. They were living in areas such as Corinth, Rome, Ephesus and Antioch, where most people were Gentiles. Some of their main problems were to work out the new relationship between Jew and Gentile, the right attitude to the authority of the Roman Emperor, the right response to pagan ways of thinking and behaving, and how to be a community in a situation where the great majority of persons were slaves.

These second Christians were convinced that Jesus was with them, as their Master and source of truth. He was with them as much as he had been with the first Christians. Nobody tried to choose a successor to Jesus! But what about the stories which the first Christians remembered, about the activities of Jesus in Galilee and Judaea? What use were they? The second Christians faced new questions, questions to which the stories of Jesus could give no answer because Jesus had never faced them. Jesus had never given an answer to such questions as 'Should Jews and Gentiles eat together?' or 'Can we eat food that has been sacrificed to idols?' Such questions had not occurred in Jesus' experience. So, for these second Christians, there was not much point in asking 'What did Jesus say?' But they could ask, 'What is the Spirit of Jesus trying to say to us now?' And so they were led to a new obedience in unprecedented situations. When that happened, they found that the older stories of Jesus were, after all, worth remembering and re-telling; they discovered the connections between what God had been doing in Jesus and what God was seeking to do through them in their new situations. So they treasured and recorded these stories: they needed the stories of the past in order to interpret and to respond to the demands of the present.

Now we are in this year of ours and in this place of ours.

Here and now, we also are groups of second Christians. We are in the same situation, fundamentally, as the second Christians in Corinth or Antioch. We, like them, face new questions, questions that cannot simply be answered by asking, 'What did Jesus say?' We are the early Church for this year. No one has ever been here before us. But we can have the same trust that they had, that the truth is not only in the past but is ahead of us, and that the Spirit of Jesus is leading us into it (John 16:13).

So we need the same approach as those second Christians of nearly 2000 years ago. We seek to discover what our Christian obedience means in our unprecedented situations. Like them, we have to start with the demand of our own situation, we discover connections between it and the stories of Jesus, and we are given a clearer understanding of the action or response which God seeks to make through us in our world.

This is why we read the Gospels. The Gospels are not intended to give us mere information, or facts about days gone by, or an uplifting spiritual experience, or a design for social improvement. The Gospels were written in response to the Church's need, as it struggled to be a missionary community committed to the programme of Christ's Kingdom. The New Testament is all about the transformation of persons, of society, of the universe. It is about Christ's programme of remaking creation so that it becomes true to the mind and purpose of the Creator. To treat it merely as an object of historical or literary study, or as a source of individual comfort, is to misuse it, to bend it from its purpose: it is like using a chisel to do the job of a screwdriver – it's bound to make a mess. The Gospels start to make sense when they are picked up by a group of people who want to be a missionary community. Only a cook really *understands* ovens: other people may get to know a lot of facts about them; but to understand them you have to use them. Only a missionary Christian can really *understand* the Gospels. This book is offered to people who want to be part of the Christian movement, putting the Gospel story to work.

In one way or another, we shall find that we are doing four things as we study a Gospel story.

1 We will identify the human motivations in the various reactions to Christ in the story.
2 We will identify Christ's judgements and responses to them.
3 We will try to identify what would make the story ring bells for the second Christians, who were the first readers and recipients for whom the Evangelist wrote.
4 We will identify linkages and connections with our own lives, as we engage with our own calling and discipleship.

We hope that this book will be of use to small groups of Christians who wish to test out and to transform their church practice and policy in the light of the stories of the Gospels. To use the stories in this way is to be faithful to the original purpose of the Gospel-writers. The Christian community refers to itself as the Body of Christ. A body is a person acting, speaking, experiencing. The Body of Christ is Christ acting, speaking, experiencing, making Gospel events, in the days of the New Testament people and in our own day. The Gospels are the record of the words, the actions, the experiences and the suffering of Jesus: they tell us what God looked like, incarnate in the person of Jesus. In the Christian community, the Body of Christ, God seeks to continue that word, action, experience and suffering in our own day.

Our basic question, therefore, as we work with the Gospels, will be: **If this is what God in Christ was like *then*, what is God seeking to do in us, the Body of Christ, *now*?**

We may expect and pray to get two things from our work of Gospel study:

1 We can see what God's action is like in the world; and from this we can get mandates, priorities and guidelines for our programme as a Christian group – healing, proclaiming, confronting and compassion-ing.

2 We can see the effects to which obedience to the Kingdom leads: we can see what God suffers in the world in the person of Jesus. From this we gain resources for interpreting and coping with the effects of our own work – the misunderstandings, conflicts of interest, clashes with authority, periods of storm, darkness and delay. Because Christ is risen, the members of his Body can face the carrying of the cross after him.

So this is the summary of our purpose in studying the Gospels:

1 To seek guidelines for our programme in the Christian movement.

2 To gain encouragement in coping with the effects and results of our discipleship.

4

A Method for Working with a Story

The chapters in Part Two of this book end with a suggested programme for groupwork. This is based on our experience. But it is essential that the group comes at the story in its own way and at its own pace. What we offer is not a set of rigid recipes. All we can do is to tell how the stories have worked for us.

What do we mean by a 'group'? In our experience, anything between six and 340 people! You will see that we nearly always suggest breaking into 'teams'. A team cannot realistically be less than two people. Usually, at least three teams are needed to represent the characters in the story, so six people seems to be a practical, minimum size of group. At the other end of the scale, we have sometimes worked with 16 groups, each made up of four teams, each team with seven members, all in one hall. It can work very fruit-fully, provided that the instructions are reasonably clear. It is much better to have a large number of small teams than a small number of large teams. If a team has more than seven people, its members will not be able to hear each other against the noise of the other teams; and not every member is likely to be able to make their point. When meeting in teams, it is important that members should be able to hear each other. We encourage them to get together in close clusters, sitting 'knee-to-knee', so it is helpful if the seating can be flexible. But this does not imply that this sort of work can take place only in a hall with movable chairs. Sometimes we do have to meet in church buildings, with fixed pews. This can work perfectly well, provided that the numbers in each team are kept small – not more than about five. If we have a total group of 50 people, and it seems right to use a story with only four characters – such as the Bartimaeus story, or the story of the ten lepers – we would break into two sets of four teams each.

The instructions do need to be clear, and members who give up their time to come to this sort of study have a right to expect good visuals, for example acetates on an overhead projector (a most valuable tool), or a flipchart, and work-sheets. But, at the same time, the leader or organizer should not give the impression that we are going through a scripted routine and that the outcome is known in advance. Even the visuals should not give the impression that they are all neatly sewn up beforehand. The leader is not in business to ensure that all the members come away possessing a fixed body of knowledge. The leaders have as much to learn as anyone else. The members must not come away with a sense of having been manipulated, or of having been on the receiving end of clever (or not-so-clever) tricks. The whole object is to set the members free to go on exploring the Gospels themselves, not to make them dependent on the leaders. One way of lowering the status of the leader is to split the role between two or more leaders. We have often presented these studies as a double-act, alternating between the different phases of the meeting. In some instances (see Chapter 17 below), this is essential. It is a good thing for the leaders themselves to be not over-familiar with the story concerned. We find that we do come at each story new each time. Over the last 20 years or so, we have probably never used any one story more than about six times. We have been doing this sort of thing very much in odd moments, and have never set up as experts in educational processes. We have discovered, time and again, that there are vast resources of theological awareness and sensitivity among the 'ordinary' people who join us in these explorations. For instance, look at the long list of points of interest in the story of Jairus and the woman with the haemorrhage. This was not worked out by one person in a study; it is the accumulation of insights from members of working groups as they have entered the story and found their voice, over several years. And part of the reason for this creativity is that so many members of congregations have had little previous opportunity to put their faith and their perceptions into words.

The groupwork in this book is an attempt to help people to be theologians, to show theology at work. As Bishop Laurie Green says, 'Good theology is more likely to derive from a problem than from a statement, more likely to arise in a prison than a palace.'[1] Such theology does not initiate; it is a response to an event of some sort.

This book is not really intended as a primary piece of work. Its basic data are in the Bible. About 15 years ago, our friend Ian Fraser of the Iona Community called a group of us to work with him on Iona on a programme called 'Theology for Living'.[2] This was a detailed and quite sophisticated process for forming theological responses to real-life situations. It depends on making a thorough analysis of a chosen situation, which is preferably a complex situation in a secular scene – an educational or industrial structure, for instance, or a dilemma facing a town councillor. It calls for a carefully checked statement of the situation, identifying the powers and pressures and human consequences within the situation. Only after this has been done thoroughly, according to a consensus of the group, do we turn to the Bible and other traditional sources, to claim symbols or models of practical faith. We do not jump in hastily with prefabricated religious platitudes. This is a truly valid theological process; people who are really involved in a situation discover ways of faith to use and to live by. That process is what we might call a primary form of theology. Our book is perhaps more secondary, a stage further away from the cutting-edge. It is complementary. It starts from the other end. Its agenda is set by the Bible itself. But the purpose is the same: to help Christians to work out something of what it means to be the Body of Christ in our immediate situation.

This book is a series of studies on the experience of 'salvation' in the Gospels. It is just a selection of possible examples. It is not a study-course. No one is expected to work through it from beginning to end. It is a quarry, from which you can select what seems appropriate at any particular time.

Human beings are sometimes said to learn by experience. This is not strictly true. Many people can have an experience, but not all will learn from it. We learn by *reflection* on experience. That is what theology is about; it comes second. First, there has to be the experience, the event. Our learning process is a loop. First we *do*. Then we move away from our

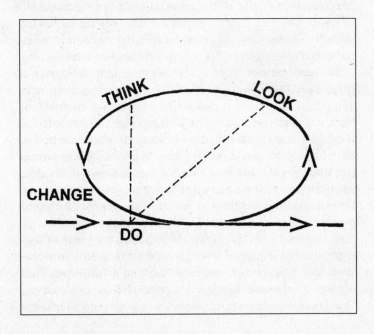

doing, and *look* at what has been happening. Then we
think about it. Then we move back into our line of action,
and either *do again* or *change*.

We apply this pattern to our Bible study. We have a long
line of *doing* or *experience*. In the Bible this starts with
creation, or Abraham or Moses. It continues with Jesus and
the other figures of the New Testament. For the purposes of
this book, the *experience* is primarily in the events recorded
concerning Jesus. In each case, there is an event within an
event. The 'event' which we actually see on the page is the
action of the Evangelist in recording the story; it includes
his motive for doing so, the way he selected his material, the
needs and interests of the community for which he was
writing, and so on. This 'faith' of the Evangelist is what the
text actually demonstrates as evidence. That is the event
that we meet on the page. Then, inside this event, there is
something that happened in the life of Jesus, something that
gave rise to the faith of the Evangelist and the Evangelist's
Church. And then the *experience* continues along the history
of the believing Church; in an unbroken process, it includes
us, in our own time and place. It includes last week.

We meet for our Bible study. We take time off from our
immediate line of action. We *look* at what has been happening, at who we are, and we begin to make connections
with the previous history of God's people, as recorded in
the Bible. Then we *think* more objectively about the text or
story; we allow it to take us where it leads. We explore its
meaning. We include in this our older colleagues in discipleship, the Evangelist, the Church for which he wrote, and
the community that found the story memorable and worth
treasuring.

We change direction again. We look to see what *change*
is required of us, as we try to discover how we are to be the
Body of Christ in our own time and place. And from there
we move back onto our line of action. We rejoin history.

It is interesting to notice how this 'loop' pattern is being

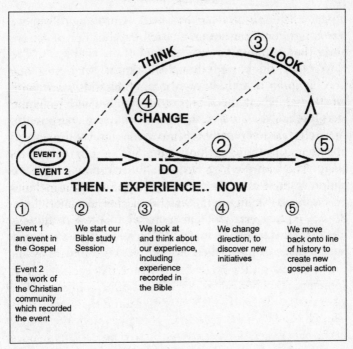

① Event 1
an event in
the Gospel

Event 2
the work of
the Christian
community
which recorded
the event

② We start our
Bible study
Session

③ We look at
and think about
our experience,
including
experience
recorded in
the Bible

④ We change
direction, to
discover new
initiatives

⑤ We move
back onto line
of history to
create new
gospel action

discovered by many different people and groups, apparently independently of each other. What we describe here is similar, for instance, to Laurie Green's pattern in *Let's Do Theology*.[3] It is similar to many traditional schemes of meditation and mental prayer. Its claiming of our imagination brings it into alliance with the widely valued practice of Ignatian spirituality.

In the Urban Theology Unit and elsewhere we have used various sets of terms as labels for our three main phases. Not long ago, I was at a consultation at which someone asked for some information about Ignatian spirituality. This appeared in the minutes as '*Ignition* spirituality'. This seems to be a good title for our opening phase of 'Looking'. So, in this book, for our three phases, we use the titles *ignition*, *exploration* and *destination*. We shall be satisfied if these Bible studies can be a sort of switch-on for local groups on their journeys with the Gospels.

In the 'Working Groups' section of the chapters in Part Two of this book, we follow this loop pattern.

1. *Ignition* is a phase of switching on and *making connections*. Here, we need to try to ensure that every member gets 'on board'. Usually, this means finding a question that will relate to every member's experience, and will give every member something to contribute. So, for instance, in the chapter called 'Getting Started', we ask people to think about their own experience of getting something started. We ask people to share their ideas, literally in twos or threes, so that everyone has a chance to say something at the earliest stage of the meeting. Or, we read the story right at the beginning and then ask people to go into twos and

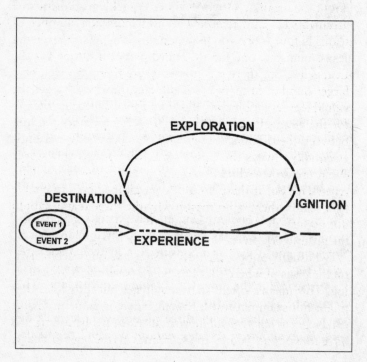

threes to share with each other what first strikes them about the story – something or someone that they identify with, something that puzzles or pleases or disturbs them. At this point, people are talking about *themselves* and their impressions; at this point, no one can be *wrong* – even if they are technically misunderstanding the text. Each person is an expert on their own history and insight.

2. Then we come to the more detailed *exploration* of the story. At this point, the story is read aloud, in the dramatized form – unless this has already happened. (We provide the dramatized text in this book, but members should be encouraged to bring their own versions as well; no translation is perfect, and that includes the dramatized version, as we have already mentioned.) The leader may need to point out the salient issues, or clarify some of the factual matters about the meaning of words, but as quickly as possible the group breaks into teams. The most common number of teams is four – one for Jesus, one for the person receiving Jesus' ministry, one for the 'third party', and one for the Evangelist. But there are stories where there can well be a larger number of teams. It is difficult, however, to get the valuable interaction with less than three. The fourth team, for the Evangelist, is very useful indeed; it makes the link between the original readers and ourselves. Its question is essentially always the same – why do you tell this story? What use do you think it is going to be for the people who receive it? But if there are not enough members to enable four teams, there is no reason why the three teams should not go into the 'Evangelist' role after they have dealt with the groupwork on the story itself.

We usually put people into these teams quite arbitrarily, on the basis of where they happen to be sitting in the meeting. This means, often, that people get put into roles that might not seem natural for them. There is value in this. It can be positively fruitful, for instance, for a 'bishop' type to have to work at 'be-ing' the woman with the haemorrhage,

or for a quiet and unobtrusive girl to have a go at 'be-ing'
John the Baptist. The members of the teams may at first
need to be encouraged to get into the *role* of the character
that they have been given, to see what is going on from that
character's point of view. We ask them to try to move from
'I think that the woman must have felt like . . .' to 'I am the
woman and I feel like . . .' Some people will find this easier
than others. It is largely a matter of people feeling free to let
their imaginations take over. If they are wrong, on an intellectual level, there will be opportunity to put them right.
Our colleagues in the group will probably cut us short if
our imagination strays off into self-indulgent fantasy; they
will be right to ask whether our picture is justified by a
disciplined reading of the text. But our imagination is still a
necessary gift for us to use in this work, and our educational
conventions do not encourage us to develop and employ
our imaginations – not after we pass into secondary school,
anyway. Without dedicated and lively *imagination*, we are
not likely to get far in the following of Jesus. Imagination,
rather than intellectual logic, is the engine that provides
motivation for most of our enterprises, for good or ill,
whether it is getting married or setting up an act of terrorism. Imagination has a vital role in our discipleship of Jesus.
This is why he so often engages us with our imagination, as
he teaches by parables. He does not tell us what to believe;
he puts a live situation before us and asks, 'Where do you fit
into this picture?'[4]

   At the same time, it is the *role* that we are looking at
(we do not usually use the term 'role-play', because that
suggests something borrowed from the stock-in-trade of
professional sociologists; there's nothing wrong with that,
but we are not in the game of any professional expertise,
which can so often give people the feeling that they are
dis-abled). The *role* is what can be transferred from one
situation and culture to another; individual personality
cannot. It might be possible to make a psychoanalytic study

of, for instance, Pontius Pilate; this could account for his particular features of weakness or vacillation or authoritarianism. But it would not help Christians who have to sort out their relationship with the law. The important thing about Pilate is not his individual unique personality but his role as a magistrate. Similarly, we might be able to ferret out the peculiar quirks of personality that made that individual 'Good Samaritan' good; but the issue for the Gospel is the role of the Samaritan, and how we see the acts of divine mercy being performed by such people. It is the role that is transferable across time and space to our own context. Who is the 'Samaritan', or the 'priest', or the 'lawyer', or the 'leper' or the 'paralytic' for us?

To help members to get into the roles, we give labels for them to stick on their clothing, to identify them. We give the teams around six or eight minutes to get into their roles, using the questions supplied. These questions are supplied on paper or on the overhead projector. On the whole, the projector is less fuss – members already have the story on paper, and it's as well not to have too many bits of paper to handle.

The device of 'visiting' is usually very fruitful. We break into the flow of the teams' discussion, and ask that each team (except the 'Evangelist') choose one or two members to go to visit another team. This is where the labels are very useful. We give the 'visitors' an opening question to ask the team that they are visiting. If, as sometimes happens, there are members who have been unwilling to make the jump of getting into their role, they find themselves spurred into doing so by the arrival of people bearing a different role. The noise level in the room usually goes up quite noticeably! There can be quite a bit of laughter and sometimes real anger, as people find that they are being obstructed by other people's presence or attitudes. The 'lawyers', for instance, in the healing of the paralytic can get quite a rough ride; and then it is necessary for us all to realize how strong is the mind of the 'lawyer' in the attitudes of many committed Christians – especially those of us who are involved in the structures and organization of the Church.

If there is an 'Evangelist' team, it divides up and goes to overhear the conversations of the other teams. This is what any evangelist has first of all to do. Mark and Luke had to be listeners. So do all evangelists. The 'evangelist' in any situation will probably be an 'insider' to the Christian community; but the faith of the insider is shaped and modified by contact with the 'outsider'. The conversion of Cornelius leads to the conversion of Peter, and that leads to the conversion of the Church (Acts 10; 11). The members of the 'Evangelist' team may well discover all sorts of dynamics in the story that they had not been aware of before, as they listen to the interaction of the various roles. After about seven minutes in this phase, the 'visitors' are asked to return home. The teams are given a couple of minutes to share what has happened, so that the 'delegates' are able to tell how they got on, and the 'home' members can describe what it was like to be visited.

Then the leader calls the whole group together for a plenary reflection. Often, this can best be started off by the 'Evangelist' saying why he thinks that the story is worth telling. At this point, all sorts of insights may emerge. The leader will probably have a kind of checklist of points that ought not to be missed; but the more the main points are provided by the members, the better. They will probably come up with insights that the leader has not thought of.

At the next stage, the leader has a crucial task. The group may well want to go on indefinitely exploring the details of the text, and sharing the experience of being in the roles. But this must stop! We must move from the there-and-then into the here-and-now. Members are instructed to remove their labels, and anyone who experienced any difficulty or hammering in their role may need a bit of affirmation.

3. We move into the final phase of the meeting: the

destination. This is the most unpredictable phase, depending on the local situation. In this book, we suggest just some of the possible practical issues that could emerge. It is essential to leave adequate time for this phase, especially if the meeting is in a local situation where some really practical planning can take place. This is what the whole exercise has been for. It means a conscious change of gear, and one-third of the total meeting-time should be set aside for it.

For the groupwork of most of the following chapters, we would normally expect to set aside a period of about 75 minutes. A shorter time would be possible, but it could feel rushed. If the *Ignition* phase takes ten minutes, and the *Exploration* phase 40 minutes, this final *Destination* phase should take not less than 20 minutes. This will show whether you have really been meaning business with your Bible study, or whether it has been just another religious exercise for the benefit of people who like this sort of thing. This is where you move from being a story-reader into being a story-maker. Only too often in a parish there is a keen Bible study group, which meets dutifully and enthusi-astically, but its existence makes no difference to the public policy and practice of the church – let alone any discernible difference to the world around it.

This is the point where you should hope to feel that you are accountable for the time and energy that you put into your Bible study. As a unit of your local church, you are accountable to that church. You should be expected to act as a think-tank or a research-team, on behalf of the other members. Perhaps you will be a pressure-group, represent-ing interests that your local church is not yet taking sufficiently seriously. So, therefore, you are also account-able to the world around, especially to the people for whom the existing systems are not working well – the dis-abled, the excluded, the people on the edge. They have a right to expect that the Body of Christ will be accessible to them, available to them, a 'first touch' to the source of healing and truth. This could be your role. So you should expect that you will be given leads and guidelines about future action; you need to make sure that these are properly recorded and transmitted. Just one small example: a couple of years ago, during a time of great concern and scandal arising out of allegations of child abuse in some institutions of North Wales, a deanery Bible study group happened to be working on the story in Matthew 2 of the massacre of the innocents. This led directly, in the following year, to a major gathering at St Asaph Cathedral, to affirm the Value of the Child. It gave an opportunity to a wide range of people from statutory and voluntary organizations all over North Wales, from the Church and the general public, to express corporate repentance for terrible damage inflicted on young people, to affirm the good, caring work done by so many people whose professions had been brought into disrepute, and to rededicate the whole community to the service of children. The issues and the needs would have been there anyway; but without the initiative of the Bible study group, the event would not have happened as it did.

So, here is an alternative version of the purpose of your Bible study: it is to change and develop the members, so that they can help to change and develop the Church, so that it can work with God to change and develop the world.

There are three faculties in the group that are needed, for the fulfilling of this purpose:

1 careful attention to the text of Scripture (this will include some willingness to discover the background in history and in other parts of the Bible);
2 lively and free imagination;
3 commitment to the task of being a disciple-group in the world.

Part Two
Stories

5

Getting Started

The Gospel Story

Mark 1:1–20

Narrator	This is the Good News about Jesus Christ, the Son of God. It began as the prophet had written:
Prophet	God said, 'I will send my messenger ahead of you to clear the way for you.' Someone is shouting in the desert, 'Get the road ready for the Lord; make a straight path for him to travel!'
Narrator	John appeared in the desert, baptising and preaching.
John	Turn away from your sins and be baptised, and God will forgive your sins.
Narrator	Many people from the province of Judaea and the city of Jerusalem went out to hear John. They confessed their sins, and he baptised them in the River Jordan. John wore clothes made of camel's hair, with a leather belt round his waist, and his food was locusts and wild honey. He announced to the people:
John	The man who will come after me is much greater than I am. I am not good enough

even to bend down and untie his sandals.
I baptise you with water, but he will
baptise you with the Holy Spirit.

Narrator   Not long afterwards, Jesus came from
Nazareth in the province of Galilee, and
was baptised by John in Jordan. As soon
as Jesus came up out of the water, he
saw heaven opening and the Spirit coming
down on him like a dove, and a voice
came from heaven:

Voice   You are my own dear Son. I am pleased
with you.

Narrator   At once the Spirit made him go into the
desert, where he stayed forty days, being
tempted by Satan. Wild animals were there
also, but angels came and helped him.

After John had been put in prison,
Jesus went to Galilee and preached the
Good News from God:

Jesus   The right time has come, and the Kingdom of God is near! Turn away from your
sins and believe the Good News!

Narrator   Jesus walked along the shore of Lake
Galilee; he saw two fishermen, Simon and
his brother Andrew, catching fish with a
net. Jesus said to them:

Jesus   Come with me, and I will teach you to
catch people.

Narrator   At once they left their nets and went with
him.

He went a little farther on and saw two
other brothers, James and John, the sons
of Zebedee. They were in their boat getting their nets ready. As soon as Jesus saw
them, he called them; they left their father
Zebedee in the boat with the hired men
and went with Jesus.

Making Connections

How did it all begin? A natural question. It would inevitably be asked by people who had been influenced by the preaching of the Apostles in the early days of the Christian movement. We all want to know where we have come from.

It is an important question. It is not just a matter of curiosity. If we ourselves are trying to get some new development going, in a new situation, we hope that we can get advice and inspiration from looking at the way in which the work of Jesus got going. That was true for the followers of Jesus in the first century AD, and remains true for us in the twenty-first century.

Matthew and Luke recorded stories about the birth and infancy of Jesus; for them, that was the beginning. Mark, who wrote before them, was content to start with Jesus as an adult, and to begin with the commencement of his ministry. But, even for Mark, Jesus does not just come out of nowhere. Something is already happening, and this provides a situation for him to move into. The 'something' is the movement led by John the Baptist.

Jesus knows, as well as any bus company, that it's no use starting where people are not and trying to take them to where they don't want to go. He starts where people are. He follows a natural procedure that almost always applies when someone wants to get something going. Whether it is a matter of starting a local Sunday School or a national political party, the leader will usually have to follow a sequence of this kind:

1 The leader will have to identify with the existing set-up, and really belong to it.
2 The leader will have to get to know the area, its people and its interests.
3 The leader will discover needs, and identify dissatisfactions with the existing systems.

4 The leader will develop personal confidence and vision.
5 The leader will sort out ideas and priorities.
6 A start will be made where there is a need or an opening, a new opportunity or vacancy.
7 The leader will have to advertise the new opportunity, and make a statement of purpose.
8 People will be challenged to take advantage of new options.
9 People are found who are available for new commitments, to take up work and roles.
10 A working group will be formed around the leader.

We can see all the elements in this process, as they happen in the experience of Jesus. Anyone who wants to start something new, as a follower of Jesus, will find that the same process happens.

So we see Jesus beginning at the beginning. Jesus has spent many years just being where people are. He is not a rootless world-citizen. He is a man, a Jew, with a Jewish background, a Jewish identity, a Jewish language, a Jewish voice, carrying in his person the insignia of a Jew in his circumcised penis. Further, he is a Galilean, a member of a northern provincial community, far from the centres of power and prestige, of learning and influence. He has the background of a self-supporting artisan family, loving the area and familiar with its ways of farming but unable to own land; familiar with the economics of production and selling and buying, but unable to make much of a living because of impossibly high rates of taxation; familiar with the problems of moving in and out of different districts administered by different authorities, each of which demands its rake-off in terms of border-tolls. When, in the next year or two, Jesus becomes a teacher, he will incorporate all these elements of his background – and many more – into his parables. We can look at his teaching and ask what subjects will have most interested him at school; the answer will, of course, include religion; but closely behind there will be botany and economics.

Jesus has spent many years just belonging. But during that time he has been preparing to make a move. All across his nation there is argument and confusion. Everyone knows that things are not as they should be. The nation has lost its independence; its land is occupied by the colonizing power of Rome; its religious leadership is tolerated by Rome for as long as it causes no trouble; its productive wealth is being siphoned off by the Romans and exported for their benefit. There are many voices, each with a solution to the problems. There are those who refuse to face the fact that Roman power and wealth are far greater than they can ever compete with, and who think that they can solve the problems by violence and terrorism and by making the land ungovernable. There are those who hope to improve matters by stressing religious values and by obeying the strict letter of the moral codes. There are others who insist that things would be better if people would just quietly accept things as they are and go along with the present establishment. And there are others who blame everything on modern commercialism and urbanization and who solve the problems by getting away from it all into the desert. All of these voices – Zealots, Pharisees, Sadducees, Essenes – make some appeal. But they all locate the problems outside themselves – the Romans, or the sinners, or those who rock the boat, or the sophisticated city people. They all depend on finding someone other than themselves to blame.

And then another voice appears on the scene. He does not tell people to lay the blame on other people; so he does not appeal to built-in hatreds and prejudices. He urges people to take responsibility for themselves, and to form a movement of renewal of themselves where they are. This is John the Baptist. He emerges from within his community; he is rather like the 'community agitator' whom Bishop Wickremesinghe of Kurunagala encouraged in Sri Lanka, a person who helps members of an oppressed community to recognize their situation and do something about it.[1]

John appears as a very traditional figure. We do not have any indication anywhere of what Jesus looked like, and only one hint (in the crucifixion story) of how Jesus dressed. But Mark tells us how to recognize John. John dresses deliberately as an old-world prophet. It is as if a man started to walk around our twenty-first-century streets dressed like the man on the Quaker Oats packet. He comes representing traditional ethical values, based in the law and the prophets of old. His morality is not a matter of rigid adherence to ritual purity, but rather of proper sharing of wealth, and of avoidance of fraud and violence. He preaches a call for repentance, so that people may be set free from their sense of guilt. This is more controversial than it may sound at first. There was an established system for dealing with people's sense of guilt, operated according to the law by the authorities of the Temple. It involved various costs in the purchasing of items for sacrifice, and in travel. John is inviting people to opt for an alternative process, which bypasses this whole system, in effect suggesting that the Temple is redundant. He is offering a different method of handling the sense of indebtedness that is the effect of sin. He offers the opportunity for forgiveness or – another way of expressing the same idea – release. In effect, he is claiming the traditional vision of Jubilee, the release from indebtedness, a new start.

An austere man, John keeps to a diet that involves no industrial interference with natural products. He comes, drawing people together as a movement of self-criticism and of renewal. It is a movement for ordinary people, not for those who are prepared to go up into the hills as terrorists, not for those who have the leisure to specialize in religious exercises, not for those who can see themselves as part of the central power-base, and not for those who have the independence to go off into the desert. It is a movement that does not depend upon people's hatred for other people, or even upon their own self-hatred. And it is to John's movement that Jesus comes, on his journey downwards, into his real world.

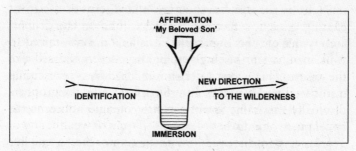

Jesus has been living deep down within the conventions and the culture of his people. And when he does make a move, he moves still deeper. He attaches himself to this old-world figure. He joins John's movement by coming for baptism. This takes him down into the waters of Jordan; Jordan with its ancient symbolism as the border and entry-point for the Land of Promise; Jordan also as an unimpressive muddy river, in the barren grimness of its valley, the lowest point on the nation's territory. Only on the far side of this immersion, immersion in the water and immersion in the culture, does he hear the new word of commissioning, the word from the Father that gives him his identity, the audible word that accompanies the visual symbol of the in-breathing of the Spirit. The experience of Jesus is a graphic illustration of the truth of the insight of C.G. Jung, 'Creative living begins on the yonder side of convention'.[2] This patient, committed process of belonging where we are is essential. In South Africa, during the development of the apartheid regime, it seemed to be intolerable. The convention of the country was so evil, so cruel in its effect on poor people, young people and children, that any hanging-around seemed wrong. But change, when it came, was brought about not by impatient firebrands who never really belonged, but by people who were deep in the scene and who suffered within it. This immersion by Jesus in the convention of his world is, for Mark, the beginning of the story of salvation.

So Jesus surveys his situation and discovers a sign of creative dissent, something stirring within the fabric of his society. He gets his own sense of calling and commitment. And then, after this high point, he goes off alone into the desert. This is not a decision reached by a lot of quiet introspection. He moves into the desert under compulsion, driven by that same Spirit who has come upon him in the appearance of a dove.

Jesus has to discover how to be alone. He has to live without landmarks. He has to be able to survive without the support of companions. He is, of course, going to be the centre of a group of disciples. He is going to be standing for all the values of community. He will in future not find it easy to be alone. But he will need to be able to continue with his commitment even when there is no human support. In the words of Dietrich Bonhoeffer, 'Let him who cannot be alone beware of community'.[3] Jesus goes into the desert, to work out his priorities and confront all sorts of illusions; Luke and Matthew give us some idea of the self-regarding fantasies that crossed his mind. The Saviour is no stranger to the possible deviations from his true course of action. He faces the beasts, the threats to his integrity. By the end of the 40 days, he has discarded the weapons that most people would have found attractive in any programme for making a difference to the world.

Then there is a vacancy in the alternative religious leadership of the nation. Herod intervenes. John has become too awkward a character for society to cope with, and Herod has him arrested and imprisoned. This is the signal for Jesus to step in. He moves into Galilee, with his own message. At first, this appears to be not much different from that of John. But John's message focused on repentance for the forgiveness of the failures of the past. Jesus brings in a new fact. The Kingdom of God is upon you. He does not say, 'Repent, or else the Kingdom will get you'; he does not say, 'Repent, or the Kingdom will not come'. His message is, 'The Kingdom is right here; turn yourself around and get involved with it'. Jesus enlarges the meaning of 'repentance'. For him, it is not primarily a matter of being sorry for what has gone wrong in the past, but of taking the opportunity that is on offer with something new. Take up a new way of thinking. The authority of God is here to take over; get into line with God. There is a real new opportunity; take it. The opposite of repentance is not guilt but complacency.

Jesus announces the direct authority of God, not mediated through the systems of religious purity managed by the temple and the priesthood. Luke, in his more extended account of Jesus' first preaching, shows how he explicitly connects his message to the old theme of the Jubilee release, the 'year of the Lord's favour' (Luke 4:14–21). This is how the Kingdom of God, the sphere of God's authority, is to break into the present situation, especially on behalf of those who get least advantage from the systems as they currently operate. This sets a theme that we can detect at many points in the subsequent encounters between Jesus and the people of the land.

Jesus starts to form his community. He calls fishermen. When we have asked people to think why he starts with people of this kind, they often say, 'It's because they were ordinary people'. True enough. He does not seek out the learned or the people of high social position. He chooses folk who will not seem to have any great advantages over the common people. But some members of a group of Trade Unionists in Finland were unhappy with the word 'ordinary'. Fishermen ordinary? They have to be highly skilled if they are to be any use. They have to be brave, willing to work unsocial hours, able to cope with discouragement, and able to work as members of a team. Their job

specification means that they are better qualified for the
role of a disciple of Jesus than most academics. 'Ordinary'?
When I was serving in the RAF, I was only an ordinary
aircraftman; but I was an airframe fitter, I was on the top
pay-grade (I was paid sixpence a day more than mere
mechanics), and I could be the specialist leader of a
group of technicians. I wasn't ordinary, and I have a lot of
sympathy for any skilled workers who do not like being
thought of as ordinary.

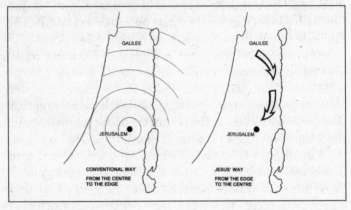

It remains true that Jesus does start with powerless,
provincial people. If you want to make a good impression
upon people of influence and status, you don't do it with
representatives who smell strongly of fish. Fish are all over
the Gospel story, from the beginning of Mark to the end of
John. Like Jesus, these first followers belong where they
are. Jesus starts in a frontier area, with people who are at
home there. Suppose he had done otherwise. Suppose that
he had gone to the capital and had selected the cream of
that year's graduates from the rabbinical school. Suppose,
then, that he had set out with these impressive colleagues,
and had arrived up north in Galilee, saying, 'Good news for
you little people; we've got a brand new policy for you,
endorsed by all the top people in government and the

universities.' It could have been an attractive start, and might have got favourable reports in the press. But it would have meant no real change to the customary ordering of society. He would have been claiming and reinforcing the existing patterns of domination and control. He might have been talking of repentance; but there would be nothing really new.

The call of the fishermen is a real sign of a new beginning in the national experience. But it is going to be a dramatic new beginning for the fishermen themselves. Jesus tells them, 'Up to now you have been catching fish. Now you are going to be catching people. You are going to have a role in society. You are going to have real influence. That is the difference I am going to make in you.' But this does not come cheaply; Peter and Andrew and James and John realize this. They commit themselves. They leave their nets. They leave their duties to their families. Jesus says, 'Follow me'; and they follow.

When Jesus calls, he calls people into salvation. But this is not just for their own sake. He calls them for a purpose. A little later in his story, Mark specifies this purpose (Mark 3:13). He gathers the team of 12 that he has called, and tells them what he wants them for. These are his aims for them:

1 To be with him; to be companions of himself and of each other.
2 To proclaim the Good News, to be communicators of his message.
3 To confront the powers of evil and sickness.

First, they have to be a team together. If we wanted to create such a team ourselves, we would probably try to find a group of people who look as if they would get on with each other and share common goals. We would try to screen out awkward characters, as if we were preparing for a '*Castaway*' project. Jesus seems to do the opposite. He creates a team of misfits. The brothers James and John are called Thunder's Kids, which doesn't suggest that they were easy to live with. He calls a recognized collaborator with the Roman occupying power, an agent of the hated tax system into the bargain, and expects him to rub shoulders with an acknowledged Zealot, a man committed to undermining the Roman authority by terrorism and guerrilla tactics. In modern church life, we would surely be able to find separate denominations for such characters to belong to; we would keep them apart. But that is evidently not the way that Jesus works. He gets the most incompatible people together and makes them a team. If they truly belong to him, they will belong to each other. Jesus' community is a miracle of salvation.

Secondly, they are called to be communicators of truth. John, it would seem, was a one-man band. Jesus is going to train a team of people to be his agents and representatives. He will send them out on industrial placements. Their curriculum as students will be in the form of a sandwich course. He will teach them, then they will go out and share what they have been taught, and then return for more.

Thirdly, when they go out like this, they will meet opposition, not just the resistance of people's ignorance and apathy but also the organized opposition of the powers of darkness, the social structures and personal destructiveness which cripple the good creation. The followers of Jesus will confront them and oppose them with Jesus' authority.

Every working team needs to have both task functions and maintenance functions. Some teams are so preoccupied with their tasks that their members get worn out and ineffective; members are valued only insofar as they contribute to the performing of the tasks, and their personal needs are ignored. In other groups, members are so keen on the gentle procedures of maintenance, of looking after each other's well-being, that nothing really gets done; members lose sight of their goals and lose interest in the whole project. In the team of Jesus, the formation of the fellowship is the maintenance function, the communication of the truth and the opposition to sickness and evil are the task functions. They belong together. Jesus is a wise manager of his staff.

A traditional 'mission station' in many parts of Africa will have three structures: (1) a church-building, representing Jesus' purpose to nourish and maintain the fellowship by word and sacrament; (2) a school, representing Jesus' commitment to the task of communication and informing; and (3) a hospital or clinic, representing Jesus' concern for the sick and his opposition to the powers of evil. These three functions represent the agenda of any team of followers of Jesus. Any local church can look at its programme and ask, how are these functions being performed, and who is performing them? Particularly with regard to the third

Starting a New Movement

Movements in General	Jesus	Us Today
Identify with existing conditions.	Born into a peasant family.	Live in the place. Be silent for a year?
Know the area.	Home in Nazareth, provincial village.	Know the bus-routes and shopping-places. Be content with being on the fringe of main-stream systems.
See where the needs are. See who is dissatisfied.	Join John's movement of repentance; getting immersed in the culture of the area; descending into baptism.	Discover people who are looking for change. Join existing pressure-group, but don't waste time with people who want to blame every-one else.

continued

Leader needs vision and self-confidence.	Jesus is affirmed as 'my beloved son'.	Leader is in some way recognized or commissioned.
Leader has to work out ideas, learn to cope with isolation.	Into the wilderness; struggling with inappropriate fantasies.	Nothing happens; a phase of emptiness and perhaps self-regarding fantasies. Work out priorities.
Start when there is opportunity.	After John's arrest.	Be sensitive for the right moment – perhaps because of an unexpected vacancy.
Need for a clear public statement of purpose. Release significant information of new intentions.	'The Kingdom God is at hand'. 'Repent' – take the new opportunity.	First announcement challenges status quo. Don't put up with things as they are. God is creating a new situation for us to work in.
A movement develops which people can join.	'Come with me.'	Find people who are available, who are not too much caught up with existing structures.
People find work and roles.	'You will become fishers of people.'	People find that they have a new significance if they join us.
Formation of a committed team.	Leaving father and colleagues and nets.	Leadership is taken by people who are not used to it; but it will be costly.

function, the answers can reveal the inconspicuous struggles of all sorts of dedicated followers of Jesus. It is all part of the ongoing programme of salvation.

So, from all this, can we recognize some guidelines for how a new piece of Christian work can be shaped? What should we expect, and what should we plan for, if we want to set up, for example, some sort of Christian enterprise in a new housing estate, or a college, or a youth group? We can refer back to the beginning of this chapter (see p. 43–44 above) to the list of things that are necessary for anything to get going; then we can compare these with the process of Jesus' own story of starting up; and from these we can see some of the elements that will be necessary for ourselves today, as we look at a new project.

For Working Groups

Ignition

Who has had experience of getting something started? It doesn't matter what, it can be a whelk-stall, a community newspaper, a WI project, a youth group, a building job, a family – *anything*. What was needed to get the project off the ground? What did it feel like?

Let members of the group share their ideas in pairs. Then, after three minutes or so, the leader can ask for one-word answers to the questions above, and write them up on a flipchart or on the overhead projector. These can be kept on one side, for reference back later in the session.

Exploration

Read the story in the dramatized form. The group leader can draw attention to the main features, especially concerning the role of John the Baptist.

Break into four teams:

1 John the Baptist
2 Jesus
3 Simon, Andrew, James and John
4 Mark, our story-teller

Questions for
John the Baptist: *What do you feel is your contribution to the process? What future is there in it for you?*

Questions for Jesus: *What are your priorities? Why do you get involved with John the Baptist? Why do you choose Simon, Andrew, James and John?*

Questions for Simon,
Andrew, James and John: *Why do you go with Jesus? Why do you think he chooses you?*

Questions for Mark: *Why do you start your story in this way? What use do you think it is going to be to your readers?*

After a few minutes, the group leader interrupts and asks each team to select one or two members to go and visit another team.

• Members from the Jesus team visit Simon, Andrew, James and John, and ask: *Why do you think I want you?*
• Members from the John the Baptist team visit Jesus and ask: *Why do you come to join me?*
• Members from the Simon, Andrew, James and John

team visit John the Baptist and ask: *Do you think that we should go along with Jesus?*

· The Mark team splits up and goes to overhear the conversations between the other teams.

When this phase has gone on long enough, the group leader asks the four teams to reconvene. After a couple of minutes for them to get together again, the leader calls the whole group together in plenary form, and asks questions that will uncover the members' feelings about the issues raised in the visiting. The leader should find that the Mark team can provide reasons for recording the story, which will lead into the relevance of the story for the discipleship of the Church in the here-and-now.

Destination

Do we see this sort of thing happening in our own day? Go back to the recorded statements in response to the first questions in the meeting, about what was necessary for something to get started, and what people's feelings were. How many of these were noticeable in your exploration of the opening story in Mark?

In your church or Christian group, are you on some frontier, some new starting-point, at present?

Do you have any new projects in mind? Go through the lists of elements in the process of getting a movement started, and see if you can get hints or encouragement from them.

Note that the one who seems to lose out most is John the Baptist. The new movement is not started without cost, pain and perhaps disillusionment (Matthew 11:2–11). Whatever he may have felt like in the isolation of his prison, his place in the whole story of salvation is secure and necessary. Is there anyone in your experience who is fitting that role?

What sort of qualifications are necessary for someone to be an apostle, which is what Simon and the rest of them became?

A word with the Evangelist

At this point, and at various places later in this book, I include an extract from an interview that might have been given by the Evangelist, St Mark, to a day-visitor at the Pearly Gates. The interviewer is Dudley, a theological advisor to a Council of Churches in a New Town in England.

Dudley	It is gracious of you, Sir, to agree to spend some of your precious time – or, should I say, your eternity – with me. I trust that I am correct in my understanding that you are indeed John Mark of Jerusalem, and that you were the first to write the Gospel story of Jesus of Nazareth?
Mark	True enough. I did put together a bit of a package. Not my trade really. But it was during a state of emergency and someone had to do it, and had to get on with it straightaway.[4] Now, if I may be so bold as to ask, who might you be? We don't usually see many folks of your type around here.
Dudley	I do beg your pardon. Of course, I ought to have introduced myself. My name is Dudley. I'm a theological consultant from the churches in Telford. I would be most grateful if you could help us with various problems that we seem to be having concerning your text.

Mark	Problems? What sort of problems are you on about? It should be straight-forward enough for a learned gentleman like yourself. All I know is we started at the beginning. Look, there, it says, 'The beginning of the Gospel of Jesus Christ, Son of God' – right?
Dudley	Right.
Mark	And we filled in the basic nuts and bolts of what it means to be a disciple of Jesus – right?
Dudley	Right.
Mark	And then we stopped when we were up to date.
Dudley	Up to date? I'm afraid that this is one of our problems. To our eyes, the ending of your story is very strange and inconclusive. Our scholars continue to have learned discussions about it. But I have to point out that our ordinary members much prefer the fuller versions that your later colleagues have given us. They feel that these succeed better in making the Gospel story complete for us.[5]
Mark	Well, let them tidy it up a bit if they feel like it. Myself, I reckon that, if you've got the message that Jesus is on his way, ahead of you, off back into all the mess of Galilee, well then, you're in the here and now, you're up to date. What more do you want? And whoever sold you the line that you can have a complete Gospel? I can't make it complete for you; nobody can. It's a do-it-yourself job for you, my friend, if you take my meaning. You get on with it, and you'll find it works.

6

Going through the Roof

The Gospel Story

Mark 2:1–12

Narrator	Jesus went back to Capernaum, and the news spread he was at home. So many people came together that there was no room left, even out in front of the door.
	Jesus was preaching the message to them when four men arrived, carrying a paralysed man to Jesus. Because of the crowd, however, they could not get the man to him. So they made a hole in the roof right above the place where Jesus was. When they had made an opening, they let the man down on his mat. Seeing how much faith they had, Jesus said to the paralysed man:
Jesus	My son, your sins are forgiven.
Narrator	Some teachers of the Law who were sitting there thought to themselves:
Lawyer 1	How does he dare to talk like this?
Lawyer 2	This is blasphemy!
Lawyer 3	God is the only one who can forgive sins!
Narrator	At once Jesus knew what they were thinking, so he said to them:

Jesus	Why do you think such things? Is it easier to say to the paralysed man, 'Your sins are forgiven', or to say 'pick up your mat, and walk'? I will prove to you then, that the Son of Man has authority on earth to forgive sins.
Narrator	So he said to the paralysed man:
Jesus	I tell you, get up, pick up your mat and go home!
Narrator	While they all watched, the man got up, picked up his mat, and hurried away. They were all completely amazed and praised God, saying:
Person	We have never seen anything like this!

Making Connections

Here we are given a story within a story. This should warn us to watch out for conflicts of interest. There are those who are supporters of the paralysed man, and there are those who oppose them.

Healing and salvation do not come without conflict, controversy and disturbance. The interests of the congregation have to give way to the interests of the outsider. The interests of the able-bodied, the vertical and the mobile, have to give way to the interests of the horizontal and the static. The horizontal take up three times the space. The congregation, intent on hearing a sermon from one who is to be known as Son of God, will not move out of the way to make space for a disabled stranger. Their religious interest makes Jesus inaccessible to those who most need him. But, when little bits of the roof start to fall on them, then they make a move. And, fair play to the congregation, at the end of the story they have changed from being a crowd of obstruction to being a chorus of praise.

Paralysis is a frightening thing to contemplate. The leper can ring a bell; the deaf person and the blind person still have some faculties and mobility to depend on. But the paralysed person is entirely dependent upon what other people can do. He or she will have to rely on people having spare time and spare energy, after they have attended to their own needs and interests.

The paralysed man would expect to be left alone, when the news goes around that the new prophet, Jesus of Nazareth, is in town. He will assume that everyone will want to go and hear Jesus, and that he will, as usual, be left out of everything interesting. He is almost correct. Most people do indeed go and crowd into the house where Jesus is speaking. But there are four friends who take a quite different line. They move in the opposite direction to the crowd. They go to the paralysed man's place; they approach Jesus only when they have collected their paralysed friend on a stretcher. They form a support-group, one for each corner of the stretcher. What does he think about this? We have no idea. We are told only about the motive of his friends.

This is a story about a journey. The four bearers make the most obvious journey. But it is a journey of discovery for Jesus also.

'Seeing their faith', Jesus is willing to be interrupted and to change direction. We are not told of any faith on the part of the patient. Faith is in the actions of the friends. What is 'faith' here? Not an invisible, rarefied quality, to be measured only by deep introspection and spiritual detection, but something that can be seen. It is not a reliance on outside intervention, but a willingness to make the most of one's own energies and initiatives. 'Faith' is in these friends who miss the opportunity of hearing a wonderful sermon, because they do not want to come without their paralysed colleague. He is their priority. And, as anyone knows who has acted as a stretcher-bearer, they have to walk in step and adjust to each other's height and strength. 'Faith' is a refusal to be discouraged; it is insistence on finding an alternative solution. 'Faith' is not a compensation for one's own inability but a commitment to vigorous, controversial and damaging action. 'Faith' is a willingness to incur disapproval and to cause real damage. The roof is only a lightweight wattle-and-daub structure, but it will still have to be mended. And who will pay?

But faith has its limits. In this instance, faith does not heal; it brings a person within range of healing. 'Faith' is a willingness to 'hand over', to 'let down', to recognize that there comes a point where we have done what we can and now it's up to someone else to take over. These friends know that they themselves cannot heal the paralysis; but they believe that the paralysis is the sort of paralysis from which release is possible. And this is a belief that Jesus can recognize and respond to. The man is let down. He can look up at his friends as he descends from them; he sees them looking down at him; their faces recede, gathered around the hole in the roof. It may feel like being let down into a grave.

Faith is in these stretcher-bearers. The men of law demonstrate non-faith. They prefer theological debate to costly action. They can try to preserve what they understand from their tradition; but they cannot heal.

But Jesus makes a strange response. 'Your sins are forgiven.' This immediately starts the lawyers off on their theological dispute. There are proper procedures to be followed for obtaining forgiveness, which have been laid down in the laws given by God. Is Jesus ignoring these? Is he setting himself up as a way of bypassing the official authorities, which people can rely on because they are traditional and recognized? A very reasonable objection. Any charlatan can come along, claiming to be able to forgive sins; if people trust in such characters, they will be in real trouble. The lawyers are in business to protect ignorant people from those who make high-sounding and unverifiable claims for themselves. Religion is a fertile area for fraud and impressive nonsense. The lawyers have a point. But they keep their thoughts to themselves. They hold their fire. They say nothing, but Jesus overhears what they are not saying. He is alert to the unspoken criticism, and he does not allow it to pass without challenge.

Even apart from the lawyers' objections, Jesus' statement seems very odd as an opening response to the situation of a person suffering from paralysis. How can a man, lying helpless on a stretcher, have sins to forgive? But this is, in fact, an essential statement about the man. Paralysed he may be; but he is still a responsible human being. If the paralytic has no sins to be forgiven, he is either perfect or he is not really a human being at all – and all too often this is how the able-bodied see the disabled. Jesus in effect is saying: 'You are more than your paralysis. You may be so preoccupied with your paralysis that you have no space in your mind for anything else – and this will keep you paralysed. But you are not a mere victim. You are a genuine person. And the first thing that a genuine person needs to know is that there can be direct access to the creative source of healing, without any guilt blocking the way. So, your sins are forgiven.'

There is something in this paralysed man that is more than his disability and more than any past action that may be trapping him in guilt. There is a genuine person there. If this fact can be asserted and accepted, so Jesus is stating, the actual physical healing is an almost trivial miracle in comparison.

So the stretcher-bearers were right. There was something in this paralysis that could be released, and the patient could be set free. The man who was let down as if he was being buried is told, 'Get up' – the same word as 'Be resurrected'.

This is a sign of God's Kingdom, the authority of God which breaks into the existing systems. There is no indica-

tion of the nature of the paralysed man's sins. There is no
suggestion that they were anything exceptional. But they
are the debt owed to God, and they inhibit his ability to live
as a full human being. The lawyers would say that such a
debt has to be paid off by means of the system of purity and
sacrifice that is provided by the rituals of the Temple. The
basis of the language about 'forgiveness' is economic. The
verb translated 'forgive' is also the word used for 'release'.
Jesus represents the direct release, the cancellation of indebtedness provided in the tradition of Jubilee. It is not part of
a calculated bargain; it is a sign of the free gift, the gracious-
ness of God which is supposed to be reflected in the deal-
ings of human beings with each other.

The effect of healing is that the patient is changed from
being a burden to being a carrier. He carries the bed that
previously had carried him. He is able to move freely and
responsibly, by his own energy. When this happens to
people, it is a sign that the Kingdom of God is at hand, that
salvation is available.

Another effect of the healing is that the man is sent home.
This is more important than it may sound. It is often noted
in the healing stories of Jesus. Sickness takes a person out of
the community. In Jesus' day, the sick were often outcast,
homeless, wanderers – most obviously in the case of those
suffering from leprosy or madness. When he heals a person,
Jesus restores to the person his or her lost rights, in the community and in occupation of the land. In the case of the
leper – the story just preceding this one – Jesus sends the
healed person to claim his rights from the public health
authority. In the cases of the paralytic and of the madman
with the 'Legion', he restores the healed person to a home
community. The sending home is a sign of the Kingdom,
the rebuilding of a broken community.

Mark has put one story inside another. The story of the
healing of the paralytic is wrapped around the argument
about forgiveness. Jesus is caught up in a conflict of interest.

He is pulled in different directions. This is a common experience of those who try to follow him in ministry, and they can take encouragement from this story. Jesus has several demands being made on him at once, and those who make these demands have interests that are in conflict with each other. Jesus has various options open to him; for instance, he could just carry on preaching and tell the stretcher-bearers to wait; or he could let himself be sidetracked by the theological argument, which could be important for him if he wants to gain public credibility with the authorities. But he decides on his priorities and attends to the paralytic.

The punchline in Mark's story is: the Son of Man has authority on earth to forgive sins. This is, indeed, a threat to the elaborate system of sacrifice by which forgiveness was supposed to be made available in Jesus' day. The lawyers were right to be affronted. There have been many attempts to work out exactly what Jesus meant, here and in other places, by calling himself 'Son of Man'. Matthew cuts through the discussion by understanding it to mean that the power of forgiveness, on God's behalf, has been given to human beings. This remains at the heart of the meaning of the story, for Mark's original readers and for ourselves. Whatever else the Church may do in its attempts to follow Jesus and to be the Body of Christ, this responsibility has a priority. The disciples of Jesus have the mandate to communicate God's forgiveness and absolution; if they fail to do so, there is no other agency on earth that has a similar mandate (John 20:23). 150 years ago, the influential Evangelical preacher F.W. Robertson expounded this story in a practical way which still should claim the attention of all who reckon that they are called to be ministers of the gospel. He disputes with those who argue that the Church and its ministers, being human, have no authority to forgive sins, who insist that this story gives the Church no mandates, because Jesus, in forgiving sins, was acting as God and not as man. No, Robertson argues, Jesus calls himself Son of Man, and in so doing he is asserting his humanity.

> It was said by the High priest of Humanity in the name of the race. It was said on the principle that human nature is the reflection of God's nature . . . The Church represents what human nature is and ought to be. The minister represents the Church. He speaks, therefore, in the name of our godlike, human nature. He declares a divine fact, he does not create it . . . If society were Christian, there would be no necessity for the Church to speak; but the absolution of society and the world does not represent by any means God's forgiveness. Society absolves those whom God had *not* absolved – the proud, the selfish, the strong, the seducer; society refuses acceptance and return to the seduced, the frail and the sad penitent whom God has accepted; therefore it is necessary that a selected body should do in the name of Man what man, as such, does not. The Church represents what God intended man to be. The Church's absolution is an eternal protest, in the name of God the Absolver, against the false judgements of Society.[1]

So this story is not given to us merely as a matter of history. It represents essential mandates for the Church as the Body of Christ in our own day.

Where are we, in the story? Are we the Christ-figure? Or are we one of the other characters? Who, in the story, is a model for the Church in our own day and in our own discipleship?

Jesus. The Church is the Body of Christ. A body is the person, acting, speaking, suffering. Jesus shows what an event of the Kingdom is like. The Church is mandated to continue to act out events of the Kingdom. The local church has to work out its policy for acting as a healing and forgiving community. It has to tell people that they are forgiven; it has to say the words of forgiveness, but it also has to act in such a way that people know that the guilt of the past no longer has power to hold them. It has to enable people to move freely, to take responsibility for themselves. How does it sort out its priorities? What kinds of paralysis are claiming its attention?

The stretcher-bearers. The Church's task is to help people to recognize and have access to Christ, not to pretend that it can do everything. Its role is sometimes temporary. It has to let people down and let people go, and not create some kind of dependency. It has to be a community of support, not a squad of fussy nuisances who keep themselves in business. It needs to work in small teams – four people may be needed to look after one paralytic. They need to walk in step with each other, and trust each other; they may have to abandon the listening congregation in order to care. They may have to do some disturbing and expensive things in order to care. Who pays for the repairs to the roof?

The congregation in the house. The Church may discover that it is fulfilling this role only too well! It can be so concerned about its own agenda that it cannot make room for those who are outside. The 'normal' make the rules and the timetables; they form the culture; they fill the place, so that the 'abnormal' cannot get in. Those who are vertical don't make room for the horizontal. They pride themselves on being able to stand on their own two feet. They are shifted only when there are problems with the roof. But, when the crunch comes, they do recognize God at work, and are prepared to praise. These rather selfish laypeople are more open to the divine presence than are the religious authorities. They will tell the story; they will watch out for the same kind of thing happening in new circumstances.

The lawyers. The lawyers, and those who would follow their example in the Church, deal in negations. Their goodness is a goodness of restraint. They would prefer to see the paralysed stay paralysed, rather than that there should be any new thing that disturbs their status and their structure. The trouble is that all of us who are in the business of running the Church as an organization are, to some extent, lawyers. We would not be ministers if there were not some element of the scribe in us. We have to keep the show on the road. And that is not just a matter of the ecclesiastical show; it is the show of education, of literacy, of health, of nationality. Every structure has its legalisms, and is in danger of encouraging paralysis and inhibiting healing.

The patient. The Church is not separated from the paralysis and sickness of the world. It is part of the problem as well as being part of God's response. Where is the Church feeling paralysed? By what? Who carries the helpless Church into the presence of the healing Christ?

The house-owner. Whose house was it? The implication in Mark's story is that it was Jesus' own house. At least, it was the place he called 'home' at the time. Who pays for the repairs? The property of the Church, as the Body of Christ, is likely to get a bit knocked around.

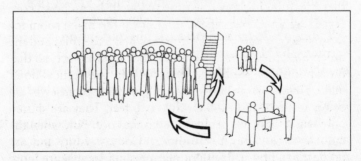

For Working Groups

Ignition

There are several issues and characters in the story so, first of all, read the story in the dramatised version.

Then invite people to say, very quickly and without forethought or discussion, who they sympathize with or identify with; and, very briefly, why. Not everyone need contribute, but give everyone the opportunity.

For instance: '*I am the paralysed man, the patient.* I know what it's like to be shunted around on a trolley like a dish of mince. I know what it's like to be carried on a stretcher.' 'I know what it's like to spend hours waiting for someone to help when I can't move' (said by a retired miner in Wrexham, who had been trapped in a rockfall). 'I know what it's like to feel totally helpless in a terrible situation' (said by a young Palestinian Christian from Galilee in 1998). 'I know what it's like to depend entirely on other people, who will give me their attention at their own convenience – otherwise, I'm on my own. I can't do anything for myself; I can't even kill myself.'

'*I am in the congregation.* I like to listen to good preaching. I resent interruptions. I resent the demands of disabled people, their noise, their appearance, the amount of space they take. I am normal. I don't like to be disturbed from the reasons I come to church.'

'*I am a stretcher-bearer.* I am not interested in sermons, but I do want to get help for my friend. I can't see the point in anything that is all talk and no action. But I know that a point comes where I just run out of ideas, I just have to hand over.'

'*I am a lawyer.* I have an alert ear for phoney arguments and high-sounding nonsense. More people get damaged by fraudulent claims than by disease, so I keep careful watch to protect the public from deception.'

'*I am Jesus.* I know what it's like to have my programme interrupted, and to have my motives constantly scrutinized and criticized by niggling, religious people. I get pulled around in all sorts of directions. I can't even be safe in my own home. I invite people in to listen to

what I have to say, and all I get for my pains is one lot
of people smashing up the ceiling and another lot
sniping at me with theological quibbles.'

'*I am the roof.* I just have to put up with people thinking
they can hack me through and treat me as expendable.'

What else?

Exploration

Break into six teams:

1 Jesus
2 The stretcher-bearers
3 The congregation
4 The patient
5 The lawyers
6 Mark, our story-teller

As far as possible, put people into the team that represents the character that they have identified with.

Questions for Jesus,
the stretcher-bearers,
the congregation,
the patient and the
lawyers: *Why are we here, in
                                      this story? What do
                                      we want? What
                                      problems do we face?
                                      Who are the problems
                                      for us? For whom are
                                      we a problem?*

Questions for Mark: *Why do we record this
                                      story? What use is it
                                      going to be to the
                                      people for whom we
                                      are writing?*

After a few minutes to discuss these questions, the teams are invited to send visitors to each other. The opening question for all visitors is: *In what ways are we (am I) a problem to you?*

- Members from the Jesus team visit the lawyers.
- Members from the lawyers team visit the patient.
- Members from the congregation team visit the stetcher-bearers.
- Members from the stretcher-bearers team visit Jesus.
- Members from the patient team visit the congregation.
- The Mark team splits up and goes to overhear the conversations between the other teams.

After a suitable length of time, the visitors return to their original teams, and the Mark team re-forms. A few minutes are needed for sharing impressions in teams, then the group comes back to plenary, and Mark is invited to explain why he tells the story in the way he does.

When sufficient time has been spent in expressing the various tensions and concerns of the story, move to the final phase.

Destination

Go back into the six teams, and think about the present day. What does this story tell us about our calling as the Body of Christ in our place? Who is paralysed? Who is helping? Who is hindering?

What are our responsibilities? For instance, do we need a transport system for disabled or infirm members? Who is keeping in touch with members who cannot get out, especially in winter? In my first appointment as a vicar in England, I visited elderly and infirm people who told me, 'I used to be a member of the parish church, but I can't continue now.' If they had said that they were no longer able to come to church, that would have been acceptable; but these people had got the sense that, because of their infirmity, they were no longer members. If people cannot come to the church, the church must go to them – the church, not just the Vicar. The church is not complete without its less mobile members. It must give these members the sense that they are valued. This can be the clearest way in which church-members can discover how to be the church outside the church-building.

Who are our stretcher-bearers? How carefully are we acting as intercessors for the people around us? What does it mean to be a community of forgiveness? Where are we feeling our own paralysis? Where are we blocked? How far are we looking for alternative solutions? Do we realize that, if we seriously try to stand for the interests of the disabled and the excluded, we shall be treated as nuisances, and that we cannot rely on doors being open for us? We may have to force access by unorthodox means.

This is a story of a journey and a process. It is particularly suitable for working out in diagrams on the overhead projector. It is also very suitable for acting out, for making a structure to represent the house with its roof. This can work well as an all-age project. You may also find that this is a suitable story for people to express themselves by making clay models, either of the stretcher or of the patient, or both.

7

The Costs of Healthcare

The Gospel Story

Mark 5:1–20

Narrator	Jesus and his disciples arrived on the other side of Lake Galilee, in the territory of Gerasa. As soon as Jesus got out of the boat, he was met by a man who came out of the burial caves there. This man had an evil spirit in him and lived among the tombs. Nobody could keep him chained up any more; many times his feet and hands had been chained, but every time he broke the chains and smashed the irons on his feet. He was too strong for anyone to control him. Day and night he wandered among the tombs and through the hills, screaming and cutting himself with stones.
	He was some distance away when he saw Jesus; so he ran, fell on his knees before him, and screamed in a loud voice:
Man	Jesus, Son of the Most High God! What do you want with me? For God's sake, I beg you, don't punish me!
Narrator	He said this because Jesus was saying:

Jesus	Evil spirit, come out of this man!
Narrator	So Jesus asked him:
Jesus	What is your name?
Man	My name is 'Legion' – there are so many of us!
Narrator	And he kept begging Jesus not to send the evil spirits out of that region.
	There was a large herd of pigs near by, feeding on a hillside. So the spirits begged Jesus:
A spirit	Send us to the pigs, and let us go into them.
Narrator	He let them go, and the evil spirits went out of the man and entered the pigs. The whole herd – about two thousand pigs in all – rushed down the side of the cliff into the lake and was drowned.
	The men who had been taking care of the pigs ran away and spread the news in the town and among the farms. People went out to see what had happened, and when they came to Jesus, they saw the man who used to have the legion of demons in him. He was sitting there, clothed and in his right mind; and they were all afraid. Those who had seen it told the people what happened to the man with the demons, and about the pigs. So they asked Jesus to leave their territory.
	As Jesus was getting into the boat, the man who had had the demons begged him:
Man	Let me go with you!
Narrator	But Jesus would not let him:
Jesus	Go back home to your family and tell

them how much the Lord has done for
you and how kind he has been to you.

Narrator   So the man left and went all through the
Ten Towns, telling what Jesus had done
for him. And all who heard it were
amazed.

Making Connections

For Mark, the world of demons was not an occult, exotic
world, distant from ordinary life. It was very much part of
a real contemporary here-and-now. People felt that hell
was very close, that the threat of devils was always hanging
over them. Jesus and his followers were celebrated, in New
Testament times, for their power to cast out demons.
According to Mark, Jesus' ministry was a head-on clash
with demons from the outset. A demon is the first voice to
recognize his identity (Mark 1:24). Christ brings heaven to
earth; he forces the powers of darkness to disclose themselves.

For the people of the New Testament, there were two
kinds of sickness. There was functional disorder, which
might be a physical or sensory disability such as blindness
or paralysis; and there was fundamental disorder, which
meant that the whole person was no longer a real human
being. This latter condition was thought of as demon-
possession. Demons could take over a person. They were
spirits of irrationality. Ordinary sickness might well be
punishment for sin; but the demons' choice of victim was
quite random, so it was not a sign of guilt. So it was possible
to make a distinction between the demon and the demon's
victim. Jesus attacks the demon with holy aggression, and
supports the demon's victim with compassion and hope.
This distinction is very necessary when we are aware of
people who are possessed by the great corporate demons

such as racial prejudice, or uncritical consumerism, or a love of violence. We do no one any good by blaming people for attitudes derived from nurturing and environment; equally, it does no good to extend kindly toleration to a destructive spiritual force. A *person* can be forgiven: a *demon* has to be destroyed. To say to a demon 'Your sins are forgiven' is to tolerate disorder, to placate evil and to refuse assistance to the oppressed and the exploited. But, in the absence of a real claim on Jesus' mandate as an exorciser, the effect on the individual sufferer is too often 'Get out' – you are excluded, there is no room for you here.

All this sounds very far away from the conventional world-view of people in a country such as Britain. The exorcism of demons is something that happens among eccentric religious groups. In our day, if we heard of someone in the grip of the sort of behaviour described in this story, we would probably wish that they be referred to a psychiatrist; and that would be a proper claiming of a form of wisdom which we believe has its roots in God's creative grace. There have been terrible stories of people being badly damaged by incompetent and persistent practitioners of exorcism. Among the mainstream Churches, Church leaders have tended to ignore this part of Jesus' ministry; and some academic theologians have encouraged us to think of the Gospel narratives of exorcism as stories from another age, which should have no authority for us today. Now, we have to acknowledge that the New Testament authors do not entirely agree with each other in the way they think about these matters. Mark vigorously reports Jesus' activities as an exorcist; Matthew and Luke tell the same stories in a more gentle way. John scarcely refers to this aspect of Jesus' work at all. Paul thinks of demons as the 'principalities and powers' that steer and oppress the human spirit in the great corporate groups of human life. For many of us who have struggled with the communal motives of such powers as racism, Paul's understanding is deeply realistic, and it makes sense to think of the work of exorcism of Jesus as an attack on the groups and themes that the victims represent. There are great suprahuman forces that oppress people, especially the poorest and most excluded of people. They are experienced as forces that manipulate people and make them victims, leaving them with no choices and no voices. Poverty, racial prejudice, the inflexible systems that trap the poorest communities in the world in unpayable debt – these are some of the demonic powers of darkness that Paul would classify as 'principalities and powers'. As in the case of this man of Gerasa, they deprive people of their homes, of their ability to share in the creation of wealth, of their place within the community of the living. Where we see such things happening, we are seeing the operation of the powers of darkness.

But these powers do not operate only on the big scale, of cosmic or global events, important though these are. For people in many parts of the world – including Britain – the language of individual or local possession by demons continues to ring true. The proper question is not, 'Do demons exist?' but 'Does this language help us to give expression to our perceived experience?' Modern, sophisticated people still find themselves using this sort of language to express their sensations of acute spiritual pain. At a time when theologians are telling us to play down the language of the Gospels and the psalms, practical therapists find it unavoidable. Unless, with the same kind of discretion that we find in the New Testament writers, we keep hold of this sort of language, we may find that we have lost the best terms in which we can speak of Christ's victory to people who are feeling the depths of helplessness and terror. The traditional role of the Bishop is to lead the Diocese in its ministry of exorcism and its attack upon the powers of darkness that corrupt and trap the human spirit. This is not the time and place for me to go into details, but I can say that, since I became a bishop, I have been required to claim this ministry more often than I have been at any time since leaving Africa over 30 years ago.

This story is set in a border-land. For the first time in his ministry, Jesus is entering an area known as the Decapolis – the 'Ten Towns' – ten cities of Greek culture and background, with pagan temples. At about the time that Mark was writing, there was some civil unrest, and the Romans quartered a legion of soldiers there for over a century. Here, there is a huge herd of pigs, unclean animals according to Jewish law, which would not be allowed in the religious heartland of Judaism. In this half-Gentile area, there is a cliff full of little cavities, which could be used as burial-places. It is a place of uncleanness and death, a fitting home for this tortured and fragmented man. He is driving himself to destruction. He rejects and defeats all who try to control him. He breaks his fetters, but in no way is he free. He keeps up a violent monologue with himself. Everything about him is valueless. This is his story, this is his song. In his own person, he represents the violence and destructiveness that faithful Jews would reckon to be typical of paganism.

The man acknowledges Jesus' authority. He takes the initiative. As at Mark 1:24, the power of evil recognizes holiness more quickly than does established religion. But when Jesus commands, there is no immediate surrender. The powers of evil put up a fight. Jesus orders the demons out; but they want to stay put. Notice how, in vv. 6 to 11, Mark gets confused between the 'he' of the man and the 'they' of the demons. The demons speak on behalf of the man; they take over control of his voice. He has no name, no identity, no will of his own. He has only the name of the demons, and they give themselves the name 'Legion'. One of the weirdest mistranslations in the Good News Bible (which underlies *The Dramatised Bible*) is to render this name as 'mob'. Mark, writing in Greek, carefully spells out the Latin word 'Legion'. The demons seem to be speaking in Latin, the language of the Roman colonialist power. A legion was anything but a mob. It was a unit of the Roman army, renowned for its discipline and professionalism. One attractive translation is 'regiment'; but even this will not quite fit Mark's nuance. 'Legion' was a unit of the occupying invader, which had taken over the land from the native Jewish people; they deeply resented it, and at the same time found themselves collaborating with it. In the language of the natives, the colonial police can, understandably, get the nickname 'pigs'. The colonizers claim to speak on behalf of the people of the land, as their protectors and representatives. I'm not able to offer a perfect translation – perhaps someone reading this can come up with one. For some folk, the most appropriate version might be 'Gestapo', or 'Security Police', or the 'Stasi'. It was with a proper sense of Mark's implications that a group of white Rhodesians said to me, about 35 years ago, 'We must make sure that our black people never get hold of this story.'

Thousands of alien forces, therefore, have established their home in the man; they have turned him into a colony; they claim the right to speak on behalf of the natives. They are onto a good thing. They don't want to go back to the cold climate of their place of origin, where they won't have the status and the servants who are at their beck and call as colonists. If they have to leave, they want to go some place where they can continue to exploit the local area. They cannot simply be let loose. They are skilled politicians; they propose a shrewd compromise. Colonists are greedy, dangerous beings. Their destructive power has to be discharged. So Jesus gives them permission to establish themselves in an alternative habitat. It's a neat solution, but this new home will not take such an invasion peacefully. The full force of the demons' destructiveness is displayed as they take possession of the huge herd of 2000 pigs, which immediately indulge in a frenzy of mass suicide. From the angle of the victims of colonial oppression: brilliant! Pigs out!

Jesus, a wandering, unlicensed preacher with no political voice or vote, is more powerful than the Legion. The military might of Rome has met its match. Christ comes to set free those who are trapped by the violence of the state. All through the story, Jesus shows that he is not deceived by the demonic appearance of the man. All that is visible is the madness, the alienation, the frightening behaviour. But, inside and behind all this, there is a real person, hidden, but truly part of God's creation. This true humanity will not be revealed until the foreign powers are out.

The man is made whole, restored to humanity. His deranged functions are restored to normality. Although the actual word is not used, this is clearly a story of salvation. But this raises the question of cost. Never mind the feelings of the pigs. The point is that they have a significant financial value. They are owned for profit. They are a source of valuable employment, in a barren region. Is one man's sanity worth 2000 pigs?

Jesus has great authority. But he cannot simply wave evil away by the sweep of a magical hand. Evil is a great power; it is not driven out by a few nice people thinking nice thoughts. Overcoming evil is a costly business. Is the cost reasonable? Is society willing to pay? Jesus seems to be recklessly careless about other people's property. In today's values, that herd of pigs would represent about £160,000. Who does he think he is?

The pig-keepers go off with the grim story of their sudden loss of employment. The general public hear of the event. They come and confront Jesus, and they find the man sitting quietly beside him, dressed and sane. The story is passed round; more and more of the people want Jesus to leave.

The general public are conservative, like the demons. They do not want too much change. They would prefer to have one or two seriously abnormal people around, to assure them that they themselves are relatively normal. It is comforting to have some conspicuously mad or bad people around; their disorder gives us an excuse for ignoring our own disorder. If they go, what is there left for us to be indignant about? We stigmatize this sort of person; we insist on a spoiled identity. We order our world by demarcating ourselves from such people; so we reinforce our own fragile sense of identity and normality. We like to have this violent man around, because he is free to break his chains; and since we would love to be free of our bondage to foreign domination but daren't, he is violent on our behalf. And now we see him tamed, domesticated: do we really want this? The power of Jesus scares us; we would prefer that the abnormal be kept away out of sight than to have the power of Jesus loose in the world – who knows, he might try to change us!

Is the sanity of one man worth 2000 pigs? Society says, 'No. Jesus, out.' So Jesus leaves. Until this insane man meets Jesus, he is outcast. For his restoration, the demons are outcast. To ensure that they really go away, the pigs are outcast. To prevent any more economic loss, Jesus is outcast.

The process is complete. The insane man's worthlessness is put onto Christ. The buck stops with him. He can bear it. He takes on himself the disorder of society – or, to use more traditional language, he takes away the sin of the world. He is the lamb – or, in terms of this story, the pig – of God.

The healed man is sent home; he has been living as a non-member of the community, in the area of the dead. He has been an exile; now his rights to a place in the land have been restored. He has been defragmented, re-integrated. This is the effect of salvation.

The healed man is given a responsibility: this is not a payment for his cure, which is paid for by society and by Christ, but it is part of the significance of being a healed person. Society has demonstrated that it is unwhole, and that it would like him to remain unwhole. Hardly surprisingly, he would like to leave these people and stick to Jesus. But Jesus, in effect, tells him: 'No, you must detach yourself from me. Do not treat me as a magical authority; you, as a healed person, need to develop a proper independence.' And, to supply him with a positive status and purpose, he gives him a definite mandate. He is to be the first evangelist. He is not healed just for his own sake. He is healed to be a sign of the Good News, to be evidence of a new state of things. In other places, Jesus often tells healed people to be quiet, and not to advertise him. But here, as he leaves, he gives this man authority to tell his story. But he is not going to be an itinerant preacher, communicating always to strangers. There are some people for whom this is a proper calling. But Jesus is, perhaps, aware of the old proverb, 'An expert is an ordinary person away from home'. This evangelist is called to represent Jesus in that most difficult of environments: home.

For Working Groups

Ignition

Either
Almost every week, there is some controversial example in the media of whether we can afford to provide some special treatment for some special patient. The leader can watch out for a suitable story, and ask for the group's opinions.

Or
Have you or your church got into trouble for doing what you thought was the right thing (regardless of cost)?

Let someone try to find out, in advance, the current cash value of a pig.

Exploration

Depending on the size of the group, break into as many
of the following teams as possible (the first three are
essential):

1 Jesus
2 The man
3 The public
4 The pig-keepers
5 The pig-owners
6 The disciples
7 Mark, our story-teller

Questions for Jesus:	*Did I do the right thing? Would I do it again?*
Questions for the man:	*Am I glad that this has happened to me? What problems am I going to face as I go home?*
Questions for the public, the pig-keepers and pig-owners:	*What do we think about what has happened? What do we think ought to happen now?*
Questions for the disciples:	*Was it worth it? Would we advise Jesus to do the same sort of thing again?*
Questions for Mark:	*What do I think my readers are going to make of this story? Why is it worth telling?*

During this phase of the meeting, you could have the following question displayed conspicuously: 'Is one man's sanity worth 2000 pigs?' (What are 2000 pigs worth in today's market?)

After the teams have had time to get into their roles and questions, they are invited to send visitors to each other. The opening questions for all visitors are: *Was this healing worth doing? Would it be right for it to happen again?*

- Members from the man team visit the pig-owners.
- Members from the Jesus team visit the pig-keepers.
- Members from the disciples team visit the public.
- Members from the pig-owners team visit Jesus.
- Members from the pig-keepers team visit the disciples.
- Members from the public team visit the man.
- The Mark team splits up and goes to overhear the conversations between the other teams.

As an alternative to the visiting process, just have a general debate, with members remaining in their roles, on the question: *Was this healing worth doing?*

Destination

In this story, it is especially important that members do extract themselves from their roles or characters, and get into the here-and-now.

Ask the general question: Does anything like this happen now? Then move on to discuss the following questions: Is our Church a healing Church? Is our society a healing society? How are the costs of healing to be met? What sort of approval should a healing

Church expect? What demons do we reckon to be at
work today? How is Christ in business to deal with
them?

Another word with the Evangelist

We continue with a further extract from the interview
between Dudley, a local theologian, and the Evangelist
Mark.

Dudley	You give us a story about demons and mad pigs, and it all seems a million miles away from where we are back home in Telford. All these stories of yours belong to your culture. Things have changed significantly since those days: we are in twenty-first-century culture. For quite a long time, some of our teachers have been telling us that we have to – please excuse a necessarily technical term – demythologize them. They mean that we have to disentangle the myth-element from your stories and discover what is universal within them. We have to apply them. We have to extract their great – yes, I must admit it – their great and universal spiritual values.
Mark	To be honest, I don't think you're all that different from us. We had the same sort of problem. There was me, a poor lad from Jerusalem, trying to put it all down in Greek, pretty much a

foreign language for me. There were the members in Rome; they had to work it out in a completely different set-up. In Rome, they didn't have exactly the same problems as Jesus did in Galilee or Judaea. They didn't have the same hang-ups about pigs. They didn't have actual Caiaphases or Samaritans either. So they had to do that de-myth bit you were on about. They had to work it out for themselves. But you don't do it by staring at the book. If you look around you, and you see that something of the same sort is happening in your own scene, you'll have done the de-mything already. It won't be myth, it'll be the real thing. Tell your friends from me: get into the Jesus act, and the myth will look after itself.

8

The Superintendent Minister and the Queue-Jumper

The Gospel Story

Mark 5:21–43

Narrator	Jesus went back to the other side of the lake. There at the lakeside a large crowd gathered round him. Jairus, an official of the local synagogue, arrived, and when he saw Jesus, he threw himself down at his feet and begged him earnestly:
Jairus	My little daughter is very ill. Please come and place your hands on her, so that she will be saved and live!
Narrator	Then Jesus started off with him. So many people were going along with Jesus that they were crowding him from every side.

There was a woman who had suffered terribly from severe bleeding for twelve years, even though she had been treated by many doctors. She had spent all her money, but instead of getting better she got worse all the time. She had heard about Jesus, so she came in the crowd behind him, saying to herself:

Woman	If I just touch his clothes, I will be saved.
Narrator	She touched his cloak, and her bleeding stopped at once; and she had the feeling inside herself that she was healed of her trouble. At once. Jesus knew that power had gone out of him, so he turned round in the crowd and asked:
Jesus	Who touched my clothes?
Narrator	His disciples answered:
Disciple 1	You see how the people are crowding you!
Disciple 2	Why do you ask who touched you?
Narrator	But Jesus kept looking round to see who had done it. The woman realised what had happened to her, so she came, trembling with fear, knelt at his feet, and told him the whole truth. Jesus said to her:
Jesus	My daughter, your faith has saved you. Go in peace, and be healed of your trouble.
Narrator	While Jesus was saying this, some messengers came from Jairus' house and told him:
Messenger	Your daughter has died. Why bother the Teacher any longer?
Narrator	Jesus paid no attention to what they said but told him:
Jesus	Don't be afraid, only believe.
Narrator	Then he did not let anyone else go on with him except Peter and James and his brother John. They arrived at Jairus' house, where Jesus saw the confusion and heard all the loud crying and wailing. He went in and said to them:
Jesus	Why all this confusion? Why are you crying? The child is not dead – she is only sleeping.

Narrator	They laughed at him, so he put them all out, took the child's father and mother and his three disciples, and went into the room where the child was lying. He took her by the hand:
Jesus	Talitha, koum. Little girl, I tell you to get up!
Narrator	She got up at once and started walking around – she was twelve years old. When this happened, they were completely amazed. But Jesus gave them strict orders not to tell anyone, and he said:
Jesus	Give her something to eat.

Making Connections

This is the biggest and most fascinating of all Mark's stories up to the narrative of the arrest and trials of Jesus. It can be deeply fruitful for a group that is seeking to work out the implications of its calling to be the Body of Christ in the here-and-now.

It is another example of Mark's technique of offering a story within a story. This points to a distinct clash of interests; we see Jesus having to sort out his priorities between rival claimants. There is a powerful set of contrasts between the two patients who demand his attention.

Start with the inner story. Here is a woman in a continuous and chronic state of haemorrhage, in constant menstruation. According to Leviticus 15, any woman was unclean and outside the community of holiness during her monthly period; she could contaminate other people; she could not relate to men. This woman is excluded from the community of holiness not just for about 60 days a year but for 365.

She has to be excluded as part of the scheme by which the respectable citizens of the religious system can be kept respectable. Her exclusion is the price paid for the people's purity. And whose job is it to ensure that she is kept excluded? Whose task is it to ensure that the rules of religious control are properly obeyed? Who other than Jairus, the ruler of the synagogue?

The woman is suffering from a disability, a problem of her health. It inevitably restricts her energies. But the religious law turns this disability into a handicap; it excludes her from social life in a way that goes beyond the effects of the disability. That is the effect of Jairus's role.

In their roles, Jairus and the woman are enemies; their interests are fundamentally incompatible. But Jairus is more than just a power-figure. He may be the boss-man of the synagogue, but he is also a father. As a father, he is as vulnerable and scared as any other father, when one of his children is desperately ill. He is in a situation where his authority is useless. He comes down the steps of his place of power and rushes to the seaside, to try to get help from a young, unauthorized field-preacher. Jesus has already achieved some notoriety as a person who has little time for the niceties of the religious purity-system, or for the authority-figures who operate it. But, in his domestic emergency, Jairus puts his religious scruples aside, and falls on his knees before this unqualified freelancer.

We can express the contrasts and comparisons between Jairus and the woman in tabular form:

The Main Characters who Seek Help from Jesus

Jairus	The Woman
He is an authority in the religious system.	She is a victim of the religious system.
He is a person of privilege in the culture.	She is rejected by the culture.
He is named.	She is anonymous.
He is socially secure.	She is socially excluded.
He is male, a father, surrounded by family.	She is female, isolated, with no support.
He is able to command attention.	She is voiceless, has to grab attention.
He claims on behalf of another.	She has no one to claim for her.
He sacrifices his public dignity.	She loses her secrecy and privacy.
He is a public person, makes a public request, gets healing in private.	She is a private person, makes a secretive approach, gets healing in public.
He asks Jesus to touch the patient.	She touches without asking.
He falls before Jesus, in anticipation of healing	She falls before Jesus, in response to healing.
His professional duty is to operate the hygiene regulations.	She, for many years, has been the victim of the hygiene regulations.
Custom and law tell him that he has the right to approach.	Custom and law tell her that she must keep away.
He searches for Jesus.	Jesus searches for her.
12 years ago, he fathered a child.	For 12 years she has had to keep away from men.
As a custodian of the religious system, he has obstructed her access to society.	By interrupting Jesus' journey she obstructs his aim of getting urgent help.

The Two Patients

The Daughter of Jairus	The Woman
She is the hope for her family's future.	She has no future, only a miserable past.
She has been living for 12 years.	She has been losing life-blood for 12 years.
She represents future hope for mothering children for the nation.	She has been unable to contribute to the future of the nation.
She is in very acute emergency.	Her condition is chronic, today is no different from any other day.
She is at the age of starting to be menstrual, her physical system coming to completeness.	She is continuously menstrual, her physical system all deranged.
Her life is being wasted.	Her financial livelihood has been wasted.
Her situation is beyond human help.	Her situation is beyond medical help.
Her healing happens when she is the centre of attention.	Her healing happens when everyone is concerned about someone else.
Jesus reduces the public attention around her.	Jesus increases the public attention around her.
Jairus refers to her as his daughter.	Jesus addresses her as 'Daughter', includes her in family.
She, the daughter of privilege, has to wait for Jesus' attention.	She, the outsider, interrupts, and Jesus attends to her first.
Jairus asks for her to be 'saved', to be given 'life'.	Jesus tells her that she has been 'saved'.
Word of healing: 'Arise' – be resurrected.	Word affirming healing: 'Your faith has saved you'.
She, the daughter of privilege, is restored to a place in the sharing of food in the household.	She, the outsider, is restored to a place within the *shalom*, the peace and justice of God.

'Faith' in the Two Parts of the Story

Jairus	The Woman
Jesus demands that Jairus must have faith.	Jesus recognizes that she has faith.
Faith is expressed in making a request.	Faith is expressed in grasping an opportunity.
Faith is the refusal to be discouraged by the fact of death.	Faith is the refusal to be discouraged by religious rules.
Faith means being willing to defy the implications of a public message and a stated fact.	Faith means being willing to defy a public attitude and disapproval.

The Experience of Jesus in the Two Parts of the Story

In the 'Jairus' part	In the 'Woman' part
Jesus perceives a word that he is not supposed to hear.	Jesus perceives a touch that he is not supposed to feel.
People laugh at Jesus.	People protest at Jesus.
Jesus brings disciples in to see.	The disciples fail to see.
Jesus has a 'prestige' patient.	Jesus is claimed by an 'inferior' patient.
Jesus insists on being the bringer of hope, in spite of being ritually contaminated.	Jesus finds himself to be ritually contaminated by the woman, and strongly commends her for this action.
Jesus brings a new life, which is not just a continuation of the old.	Jesus brings a new life, in which the old laws of exclusion no longer have authority.
Jesus brings new life and hope to a young woman who can be a source of life for her family's future.	Jesus brings new confidence and identity for all women.

Jesus brings 'salvation' to the child of the privileged, a salvation which has first been gained by the unprivileged.	Jesus allows himself to be delayed by the apparently non-urgent claims of the unprivileged.
Jesus is in control, decides how to use his energy.	Jesus is not in full control, his energy is stolen.
Jesus excludes the professional people whose job it is to publicize death.	Jesus includes the anonymous victim of a system of exclusion which depends on the threat of publicity.

The two patients need each other to point up their two situations. The woman has been in her condition – excluded, disinherited – for all the years during which Jairus's daughter has been growing up to be a nice, acceptable member of the society of the inheritors.

Jairus is so obviously the person in extreme need. Everyone will sympathize with him. And yet, during these last precious minutes while his daughter's life hangs in the balance, while all the ambulance sirens are wailing madly, he has to cope with this unreasonable delay, caused by a woman who could so easily hang on another few hours.

Why does Jesus allow himself to be diverted? Why does he not tell the queue-jumping woman, 'Look, I'm very busy now. Come back on Monday'? Because, in his eyes, the woman's condition is not less urgent than the condition of the girl.

If he had not allowed himself to be diverted, the woman would not have been brought out into the open; she would not have been required to put herself into words; she would not have come to realize that her unlawful, surreptitious adventure of touching Jesus' clothes was in fact just the sort of defiance of convention that Jesus needed to enable healing to take place; she would not have heard that her action, which she rightly thought would be condemned by religious opinion, in fact won Jesus' praise. Moreover, if she had not been thus brought out into the public, we would not have been able to hear of this definition of faith; and if we had not been given this clear evidence of Jesus' approval of her action, we would not have the mandate to destroy the whole mythology of uncleanness which the woman represents.

Jesus has to have time to announce his pleasure and commendation at her unlawful action: by so doing, he knocks away a taboo which still has its lingering power where religion is part of a system of domination of women by men. He takes time to treat her as a responsible human being; she is not just a piece of property, a problem or a statistic.

In that culture, quite irrespective of her particular illness, this woman would have had little personal status. She would have had no initiation ceremony into the national community, and no access in her own right to the place of holiness. Jairus's daughter can have access to the source of healing by way of the authority of her father; the woman has no man to legitimize her access. But she has the nerve to claim such access on her own, in this furtive way. At the risk of causing her a terrifying level of embarrassment, Jesus affirms that she has every right of access to himself.

We remember a Malawian woman saying, 'I see very clearly the difference between the two patients: it's the difference between being ill at home and being ill in hospital. In hospital, all the details of your body are public knowledge.' Indeed, the woman's experience is very embarrassing; but the embarrassment was a necessary part of the Gospel event. The woman would much prefer to remain hidden. Her great fear is to be exposed, to be cut away from the place that gives her safety within the general crowd, to be isolated and made conspicuous. But in calling her out, Jesus is not isolating her; he is calling her into a community of salvation.

The woman's way of life, especially for the last 12 years, has been dominated by the belief that uncleanness is contagious. There is good authority for this (Haggai 2:10–13).

Jesus steers by a different star. According to the Law, this woman, especially after such a long period of uncleanness, is supposed to go to the Temple and make a sacrifice, in order to claim her cleansed status. Jesus makes no such suggestion. He himself is the guarantor of her saved-ness. He makes sacrifice and temple redundant. Jairus would inevitably think that contamination had passed from the woman to Jesus. But Jesus is conscious of a flow in the reverse direction – power has passed from himself to her. For him, it does not matter whether uncleanness is contagious. The important thing is that holiness is contagious – or, to quote the song made deeply true by Desmond Tutu, 'goodness is stronger than evil, life is stronger than death'.

So it was essential for Jesus to allow himself to be interrupted and delayed. But the crisis of Jairus's daughter's approaching death is not slowed down during the delay. She reaches the crisis and passes it. There is no nick-of-time rescue. The one who is secure in religious identity is allowed to die, while priority is given to the one who is insecure. Only on the far side of death is there new life and hope for the secure. And Jairus has to allow his daughter to be attended to and touched by a man who has been contaminated by contact with someone whom he, Jairus, is supposed to keep out. Jairus, at a moment of high personal crisis, has to recognize that God is not in business to fit in with our priorities.

Faith is necessary for both healings. Faith is there, unbidden, in the insecure, rejected woman. Faith has to be bidden and encouraged in the privileged man. And the faith that is required of him is much the same as the faith commanded in the woman – a faith to accept that the woman's contact with Jesus does not disqualify him from being a source of the healing power of God. And Jairus evidently does have such faith. He allows Jesus into his house. He lets him touch his daughter – itself a dubious action, in that culture; he does not discourage Jesus from incurring further contamination by touching a dead body. He sees that Jesus can take responsibility for his own holiness.

To the woman, Jesus says, 'Your faith has saved you' – and the verb has the combined meanings of saving and healing. He does not claim that he has healed and saved: your salvation is your own responsibility. What has happened to the woman is due to her own initiative. He is conscious that energy has been withdrawn from him, because he has not planned that expenditure of energy; it has, in effect, been stolen without his permission. If he were making all the decisions himself, as he does in his dealing with Jairus, his loss of energy would not have been a surprise; he would, as it were, have been budgeting for it. This seems to me to be true to experience; pastors and other carers can tell us whether it rings true to them. If we are truly accessible, we shall find that people tap into our energy without our consent. We shall be available for them to make 'the first touch'.

Jesus does not claim credit for the woman's healing. And in the healing of Jairus's daughter, he avoids publicity. He who is keen to include the excluded, here excludes those who make a public demonstration of their interest in tragedy. He is not trying to prove anything. He does not earn a living this way. He wants no publicity. But he is the bringer of the Kingdom. Where he is, healing happens. He is in the world where people are, with a hem of a garment that people can touch.

But this is not just a story of the reversal of fortunes. It is not simply a matter of the poor being raised up and the rich being sent away empty. The daughter of the Jewish leader gets her salvation; she also is restored to a place in the community – but only on the far side of the restoration of the person who has been on the outside for so long.

We might well ask, did our old brother, Mark, who has given us the story, understand all the implications and contrasts that we are extracting from it? Is this what he intended? Probably not, in every detail. But he does tell us, throughout his Gospel, that Jesus comes as one whose qualifications are suspect, and who is continually putting question-marks against the exclusive purity-system of the religious authorities. Why so? By the time that he was writing, the Christian movement was already dominated by Gentiles; a lot of the problems that Jesus faced were no longer relevant. So does Mark tell us this sort of story simply because he is a historian and wants to give us accurate information about the past? Or is it because, in these new circumstances, the Church was nevertheless in danger of becoming a religion of exclusiveness, preoccupied with a whole new set of regulations and qualifications?

For Mark and his readers, this complex story would have been very close to home. How can it be right, Jewish Christians must have said, for the claims of outsiders who have been in the darkness for centuries to be treated as urgent, while the pressing needs of Jews seem to be ignored? And the answer came, that those who are inside are continually having their situation reshaped by those who are outside (see Romans 8–11). The daughter of Judaism had to die, and had to be raised again into a Church deeply modified by the Gentile mission. And the daughter of yesterday's Church may have to die, to be raised again in a community that has been re-shaped by new arrivals. So, what might be the implications for us in our own day?

1 *For the 'insiders'.* We hear the same anxieties within the contemporary Church. Where are the priorities? With those who have been in the Church for generations, or with those who by one means or another have been kept out? And the same problems apply to the clashes of interest between rich and poor, old and young, workers and unemployed, host community and immigrants. The answer is that those who are inside get divine attention, which has been given first to those who are outside.

2 *For the despairing.* Those who are inside will come to

the point of saying, 'There's no use bothering now, we lost our chance, God has no time for us, there's no future for us, the bearer of fertility for new generations is dead. There is no new womb coming along, no one new to bleed in preparation for new life, no new source of milk and caresses to renew a springtime for our people. Our 12-year-old girl is dead, and all we can hope for is to grow old and see the place taken over by strangers.'

But, in the presence of Christ, there is no room for the professional mourner, for the person who insists on drawing attention to all that has been going wrong. Christ says, 'Don't weep; and don't mock, either. Believe the strange timing of a God who is master of his delays, whose priorities are not perverse, who is not merely trying to curb the impatience of the privileged. Have faith in one who overcomes the divide, who brings the privileged and the unprivileged into a common fellowship of the healed, with the unprivileged leading the way. Have faith in one who will come to attend to you when he has been contaminated by contact with someone whom you could not attend to. The daughter of religion has to die, and is raised into a new world of salvation where the healed alien is there before her.'

3 *For the impatient.* The Church, locally and nationally, may be longing for new life, yearning, acting and searching for it. But there may have to be a delay before we can hear the call to us, 'Child, arise', before we can eat in the new hope. Maybe we have to wait, because first of all there is someone else waiting, someone bleeding outside, waiting for a hem of a garment to be available to touch.

For Working Groups

Ignition

This is a very rich story, and the group leader will be able to think of various ways in which the experience of people in the story can connect with the experience of members of the group, such as: How do you cope with interruptions? What is it like to be shown up in public? How do you cope with emergencies and delays? What do you feel about people who jump queues?

Exploration

More than usual, this story needs to be read aloud, thoroughly and in *The Dramatised Bible* form.

Most of the detail of the story should emerge during the work in teams, so the introduction by the leader should not be too long. But before members break into teams, the essential tension between Jairus and the woman needs to be discovered, as suggested in the first few paragraphs of the commentary above. It is best not to give people the long list of contrasts at this stage; it would short-circuit the discoveries that members will be able to make for themselves. But it might be useful to distribute it to members later in the study, or right at the end.

The story is about journeys: Jairus's journey to Jesus; the woman's approach to Jesus; Jairus's and Jesus' journey being interrupted by the woman's demand; the final journey of Jesus, Jairus and three disciples to the house of Jairus. This can be expressed by sketches on paper or the overhead projector, by members of the group working it out on the floor of the meeting-place, or on a board with draughtsmen.

Break into four teams:

1 Jesus
2 Jairus
3 The woman
4 Mark, our story-teller

Questions for Jesus,
Jairus and the woman: *What are the problems that I face? Who is the problem for me? For whom am I a problem? What do I understand by the words 'faith' and 'save'?*

Questions for Mark: *Why do I tell this story? Especially, why do I tell it in this particular way? What use is it going to be for the people that I am writing for? What do I understand by the words 'faith' and 'save' in this context?*

Another team can, if you want, get into the experience of the disciples. Another could look at the experience of the daughter (one group who did this came up with the comment: 'I am the daughter; this man comes to me and tells me to get up. Adults have been doing this to me every morning for as long as I can remember. What's new?').

After each of the teams has explored the experience of their particular character, they can visit each other. The opening question for all visitors is: *In what ways am I a problem for you?*

- Members from the Jesus team visit Jairus.
- Members from the woman team visit Jesus.
- Members from the Jairus team visit the woman.
- The Mark team splits up and goes to overhear the conversations between the other teams.

After a few minutes, the visitors return to their home teams. The Mark team re-assembles, and prepares to share its answers to the questions that it has been considering.

Destination

Who is the Jairus-figure in our scene? Who is the woman? Who is waiting? Who is experiencing delays?

If we are the Body of Christ, where are our priorities? Are we facing the same sort of problems as Jesus did in this story?

How far is our religion, or our social system, an obstruction to people?

Do we make disabilities into handicaps? (If a person is severely lame, that is a disability; it is a problem that they live with. But if a church is constructed with a long flight of steps at the entrance, that makes the disability a handicap; that is the church's problem. If a person is profoundly deaf, that is a disability; if an insurance company refuses to accept payment by cheque and insists on payment by telephone and credit card, that turns the disability into a handicap.)

9

The Foreign Soldier's Prayer: 'Only Say the Word'

The Gospel Story

Matthew 8:5–13

Narrator	When Jesus entered Capernaum, a Roman officer met him and begged for help:
Officer	Sir, my servant is sick in bed at home, unable to move and suffering terribly.
Jesus	I will go and make him well.
Officer	Oh no, Sir. I do not deserve to have you come into my house. Just give the order, and my servant will get well. I, too, am a man under the authority of superior officers, and I have soldiers under me. I order this one, 'Go!' and he goes; and I order that one, 'Come!' and he comes; and I order my slave, 'Do this!' and he does it.
Narrator	When Jesus heard this, he was surprised and said to the people following him:
Jesus	I tell you, I have never found anyone in Israel with faith like this. I assure you that many will come from the east and

	west and sit down with Abraham, Isaac, and Jacob at the feast in the Kingdom of heaven. But those who should be in the Kingdom will be thrown out into the darkness, where they will cry and grind their teeth.
Jesus (to Officer)	Go home, and what you believe will be done for you.
Narrator	And the officer's servant was healed that very moment.

Making Connections

I was called up into the RAF at the end of the war with Japan. Unlike most of my fellow-recruits, I had stayed at school until the age of 18. Because of this, I was urged to become an Officer Cadet and go for a commission. That held no appeal for me. I wanted a proper job – as I saw it – and to get a technical trade. So I become a Flight Mechanic and then a Fitter, and felt thoroughly at home. After three years, I had to face a major decision. I was very much attracted by the prospect of staying on in the RAF. I still had no desire to become an Officer. In the eyes of men like myself, the non-aircrew officers seemed to be living in a faraway world, in invincible ignorance of the real job. We saw little of them and thought less. The men we really respected were the technical Senior NCOs. They nearly all seemed to be wise, experienced, competent, just and humane. I thought that if I stayed on I could widen my experience and qualifications and end up as a Sergeant, or even a Flight Sergeant. What could be better? But I was also beginning to get a weird idea that I might go and be some sort of Christian missionary, probably in Africa. And that is what eventually happened.

But I still carried with me a sense of great respect for sergeants. So I am fascinated by the centurions in the New Testament. We know very well that Jesus and his friends lived under the oppression of a Roman army of occupation. For the average Jew, the Roman soldiers were, if not exactly fascist pigs, certainly not a favourite part of the landscape. For many years, Jewish people had seen the army of Rome as the very presence of the devil. The power and greed of Rome lay behind the structures that burdened them with high taxation. The terrorist tactics of the Zealots made a genuine popular appeal. And yet, in the New Testament, from the beginning of Matthew to the end of Acts, there is one category of people for whom there is never a bad word – namely, the centurions. There is not a rotten apple among them.

This can hardly be because the Gospel-writers wanted to get on the right side of the Roman authorities. If that was their aim, they would have tried to butter up the officers higher up the tree, like the Tribunes. The status of centurions was not very high, although they were the backbone of the army's system of discipline. They were men who had risen through the ranks, from the working-class of their day; and within the ranks of the centurions there was a subtle hierarchy of status. Each of them was, normally, in charge of a century, 100 men. So the centurion's status was close to that of a senior NCO.

So we meet this centurion – the correct translation of the word given as 'officer' in our text. He comes to Jesus with his tale of woe. And then comes another Greek word, *pais*. The normal translation for '*pais*' is 'boy'. It can carry the various meanings that 'boy' has in English, and our translators have to make the best of it according to their wisdom. 'My boy' can mean 'my son'. But there is a different and specific word for 'son', and neither Matthew nor Luke uses it in this story. (In Luke's version, Jesus and the centurion do not actually meet, but communicate with each other by means of the friendly colleagues whom the centurion has invited to help him. These include local Jewish elders, and one of the remarkable features of the story is that these Jews have such a high regard for the integrity and generosity of this heathen professional soldier. When they refer to the patient, they speak of the centurion's 'slave'; but when he himself speaks, he refers to him as his 'boy'.) '*Pais*' can mean 'my servant' – colonial people can still be heard speaking in a demeaning way of their native 'boys' and 'girls' (but it does not mean 'my slave' – when the centurion speaks of the person who does what he is told to do, he uses the specific word for 'slave'). It can mean 'my boyfriend', with the implications that that could have for the relationship between an older man and a younger man. Jews would disapprove of any sexual relationship of that kind, but it was common and acceptable among the colo-nizing Romans, between army officers and their domestic order-lies. Luke speaks of the deep affection that this centurion has for his 'boy'. Jeffrey John is surely correct in his comment:

> The probability that the relationship was homosexual would not have escaped Jesus, Matthew or Luke, and in view of Jesus' systematic inclusion of so many other categories of person who were declared to be 'unclean' or 'abominable' under the Leviticus rules, it is a real question whether we are meant to see Jesus deliberately 'including' homosexuals here as another category of the despised. Certainly there is no sign of anything but approval on Jesus' part for the centurion and his remarkable faith, nor any hint of 'Go, and sin no more' after his servant is restored to him.[1]

The centurion, like the sergeant, is a man in the middle. His authority does not come to him naturally, by the accident of being born into the power-bearing minority. He is not one of those who have the look in their eyes that tells us that they have been bred to be obeyed. He has had to work for his rank, in competition with others. He is half-way between those who have never known the state of having power and those who have never known the state of not having power. He is in the midst of power, and must understand how it works. He is the middle-class.

We should not be too dismissive of the value of the middle-class. Where there is a strong middle-class, people have power and status, but their place in society is determined by their function rather than by their ancestry. They can easily become ridiculous or cruel. They can allow themselves to be sucked into the ruling system, by being manipulated and used as an instrument for subduing the powerless. But they need always to be conscious of the power and role that they exercise.

Christianity is sometimes ridiculed as a middle-class religion. At its best, this is no bad thing. Its gospel insists that the status into which we are born is unimportant, that the essential fact about each of us is our sharing in the common humanity that Christ has taken as his own. Christianity is uncomfortable for the established aristocracy; it may also be suspected as undermining the solidarity of the powerless majority. The person in the middle gets into trouble from both sides. The man in the middle is, typically, the sergeant.

So here we have this centurion. He is the first person to approach Jesus on behalf of someone else. The story in Matthew comes immediately after the healing of a leper. This has shown that Jesus is willing to disregard the rules concerning purity and defilement, in order to meet human need. The healing of a leper leads to the healing of a Gentile. And the story of the healing of the leper, itself, follows on from the Sermon on the Mount. In his teaching, Jesus has shown that he is very different from the conventional religious teachers who base their authority on their ability to support their teaching with authoritative quotations. His teaching can stand on its own; it needs no authentication from outside.

The teaching with authority; the touching of the unclean leper; and then the approach of the centurion – the centurion is able to see in Jesus a genuine authority and a genuine caring. As a middle-class man, he recognizes that Jesus is a man with an authority in his own right, not depending on ancestry or tradition. As an outsider to the community of religious faith, he recognizes that Jesus is prepared to give the same care to a Gentile that he gives to a leper. Recognizing Jesus in this way, he has the courage to state his problem.

'Sir,' he says, 'I have a boy at home lying paralysed in terrible pain.' He makes no specific request; yet his statement is a genuine prayer; he places his anxiety before Christ, in faith that Christ will make an appropriate response. Jesus immediately shows that he is, in fact, willing to incur another ceremonial defilement by entering a Gentile's house. But the centurion states that this is not necessary. 'I am not good enough for you to come to my home; and I believe that you do not need to do so. You have power over this illness, and your word can cure it from this distance.' A modern person might be embarrassed by all this, and say, 'Nonsense, your house is quite good enough for me; I insist on coming.' Jesus elsewhere does not refuse to enter a Gentile establishment (John 18:28); but here he lets the centurion continue, for this leads to a most significant statement of faith. 'I recognize genuine authority when I see it,' says the centurion. 'I know what it means to be responsible to a higher authority: I know what it means to exercise authority over other people; I am used to giving orders and having them obeyed.' He might have gone on to say: 'I can see the difference between authority that is taken for granted and authority that is used responsibly. There is a kind of authority that belongs to the privileged man because of his birth and guaranteed status, and he will use it to support the system that gives him that status; and there is a kind of authority that a man uses not for his own prestige or benefit but to serve the community as a whole. I see all around me, in this very exclusive and stratified society where I have to work, examples of the first type. But I have come to see the value of the second type, and this is what I see in you, Sir. So I can trust you as I cannot trust these others.'

Such trust is a powerful and responsible kind of faith. Jesus says to his companions: 'I have never come across faith as significant as this before, certainly not in the traditional community of faith, the people of Israel.' And he goes on to say that those who rely on their inherited status as members of the national community will find themselves thrown out, and their place taken by all sorts of strangers from all over the world, strangers who will know nothing about the purity regulations of the people of Israel.

Jesus does not know everything in advance. Here is an occasion when he is genuinely surprised. He is not saying, 'What a lot you have learned from me.' He is saying, to this professional man of violence, with his alien identity and questionable relationships, 'What a lot I have to learn from you. In you, I have met someone who is knocking away some of the most important definitions that I have been brought up with.'

The Kingdom is being opened. Salvation is being made available across the great barrier between Jew and Gentile, a barrier not only of race but also of culture and morality. Membership of this Kingdom is to depend not on having the right parentage or the right culture, or even the right behaviour; it will depend on having the kind of faith that the centurion has. He has understood the kind of authority that applies in God's Kingdom. For those who have been brought up to take their authority for granted this will be a painful thing to accept. Healing is possible when a person has this sort of faith. And the healing is not just the healing of an individual but the healing of one of the great human divides.

In *The Man Born to be King*, Dorothy L. Sayers portrays one man, Proclus, first as the Roman official in charge of security in and around Bethlehem at the time of Jesus' birth, then as the centurion in this story, and lastly as an old soldier reluctantly on emergency duty at the crucifixion of three convicts on Good Friday; and he ends up confessing that 'this was the Son of God'.[2] An attractive dramatic idea, and historically not impossible. This is a story of how 'faith' works. You cannot prove anything from it; you cannot organize it to fit into your agenda. But, as we come to the table of the Lord, to share in the cup of our salvation, we recognize that this pagan soldier is there in the procession before us. 'Lord, I am not worthy to receive you, but only say the word, and I shall be healed.'

For Working Groups

Ignition

Prepare, in advance, for someone – preferably a member of the group – to describe their experience of being midway in an authority-system. The person could be, literally, a sergeant of the Armed Services or the Police, or a Deputy Head, or a Nursing Sister, or, perhaps, a Rural Dean. What are the problems, advantages, motives, ambitions, dangers . . . ?

Exploration

The group could divide into teams of between four and seven members, not to get into roles but to look at various questions which arise out of this story, such as: *Who do you think is a 'centurion'-figure for us now, in*

*our area? Have we seen examples of the healing grace of
God being granted to people who seem to be outside
the conventional community of faith? Why? Does it matter to you what sort of relationship existed between
the centurion and the boy? What do you think of the
authority-system of the Church? Is it healthy? Does it
give an opportunity for people who are outside the conventional authority-systems of the world around to have
a contribution and a voice? Have you been surprised by
the faith or attitude of someone who is a stranger to your
own way of life?*

Let one team take on the role of Matthew, and ask:
*Why is this story going to be valuable to my readers?
Who is going to be affirmed by it, and who is going to be
challenged by it?*

What other questions seem to you to be raised by
the story? Before the end of this phase, let each team
prepare a single-sentence statement of an important
issue that arose out of their discussion.

Destination

Stay in the teams, but let each team send one or two
members to another team to share the one-sentence
message that they have prepared; in each case, let the
receiving team consider and evaluate what they are
being offered, and, if they see fit, adopt it as their own.
Let these statements be written up on the flipchart, so
that at the end of the meeting members of the whole
group can go round and get a feel of the thinking of the
meeting as a whole.

What about the authority-system that is operating –
consciously or unconsciously – in your own group? Who
controls? Who is unheard? How are decisions made, for

instance about time-keeping? Are there improvements that you can make in the group for which you have some responsibility? And, if you have been able to make some careful judgements about this group, what about the procedures of your church?

Another word with the Evangelist

A further extract from the interview between Dudley and Evangelist Mark.

Dudley	Could you perhaps tell us how you yourself first got involved in the story of salvation?
Mark	It's still not an easy thing for me to talk about, but I'll try. Put it this way.[3] One of the first people I wanted to meet was that African lad, from Cyrene, Simon, him that carried the cross on that terrible morning. I wanted to tell him that I ought to have been there with him. But the Roman pigs got me first. I'd turned in early that evening, and then I hear all sorts of shouting and confusion outside our little place in Jerusalem. So I wrap myself up in the bed-sheet, for decency, like, as a proper Jew, and I creep out to see what's going on. Bright it was in the moonlight, and Jesus was there, and what looked like half-a-legion of security-police all around him. I had in mind to go with him, but this mas-

sive Roman head-banger caught me
first. He gets me in a half-nelson, me
being just a pint-sized pimply in those
days. He . . . he whips my sheet off me
and chucks it across to his pal. He
leaves me with nothing to cover my
manhood with, you know what I mean.
And . . . and . . . he stares at me down
there. And I'm scared as hell, and wondering what he's going to do with me
next. But he just laughs like a drain,
he does, that great baboon with a four-
inch foreskin; and he shoves me away,
and he tells me, 'You run along to
Mummy, little Jew-boy, and keep
yourself out of trouble in future.' So
what can I do? I scarper off back home,
naked as a blind herring. I don't half
get a tear-off from my mam. 'You
watch out,' she yells at me. You go
around like that and those bleeding
heathen will get you for one of their
fancy-boys. And where do you think
I'm going to get another sheet from?
That was best linen, that was, and it
doesn't grow on trees, you know.'
Moonlight still gives me the creeps.

Dudley	So it *was* you! You did interpolate that piece of autobiography into your text.
Mark	Well, I felt I had to be honest, if you take my meaning. But I don't think anyone else will have picked it up. Improper, they'd call it.
Dudley	With due respect, Sir, I think they

would be quite correct. I myself don't
feel that I can report all this back
home. Some of my colleagues would
consider it very distasteful. May I
point out that we are looking for *theology*, not for the sort of reminiscences
that are best kept out of the papers.

Mark Distasteful? You can say that again.
I've never been so embarrassed in all
my life, before or since, and never so
scared, neither, and I've been around a
bit. To be seen like that, for a decent
Jew like me, it's terrible, and to be
seen by a Gentile makes it all the
worse. It's a bit of a taste of what it's
like to be crucified. Say what you like,
I couldn't have left out that story
about me and the sheet. It's too much
part of me.

You gentry spin out your ideas
about what salvation means; well, this
is what folks like me have got to come
to terms with. We've got Paul going
around, telling us that it doesn't matter any longer what a man looks like
down there. Circumcision or uncir-
cumcision no problem, in *his* book.[4] He
says that's what salvation is all about.
'Where does he get that from?' I've
said to myself. The Master didn't have
anything to say on those lines – or did
he? A long-sighted one, that Paul. Him
and me, we've had our ups and downs.
But he's right, of course. The Master
didn't put it in as many words; but

look how he treated that centurion, and all sorts of other types that the holy growlers would call 'unclean' or 'foreskins' – or worse. I reckon it's the same sort of thing as Jairus had to get his mind around. So, good for Paul, I say. But it doesn't come easy to a lad like me. I still curl up a bit when I think of what those perishing Roman guys carry around between their legs – *and* where they put it, when they get half a chance.

Dudley   I still think that all this is quite unnecessarily unpleasant. Most of us would prefer to conduct our theological studies without going into these matters in such concrete terms.

Mark   That's your privilege; but you haven't caught my drift. Believe you me, I'm not playing games. This sort of issue is the real world for the likes of me; this is where it bites. You people, you have to work out what it's all about in *your* real world. I reckon it won't be any easier for you.

10

The Prayer of Defiant Access

The Gospel Story

Matthew 15:21–28

Narrator	Jesus went off to the territory near the cities of Tyre and Sidon. A Canaanite woman who lived in that region came to him:
Woman	Son of David! Have mercy on me, sir! My daughter has a demon and is in a terrible condition.
Narrator	But Jesus did not say a word to her. His disciples came to him and begged him:
Disciple 1	Send her away!
Disciple 2	She is following us and making all this noise!
Narrator	Then Jesus replied:
Jesus	I have been sent only to the lost sheep of the people of Israel.
Narrator	At this the woman came and fell at his feet:
Woman	Help me, sir!
Jesus	It isn't right to take the children's food and throw it to the dogs.
Woman	That's true, sir, but even the dogs eat the leftovers that fall from their masters' table.

| Jesus | You are a woman of great faith! What you want will be done for you. |
| Narrator | And at that very moment her daughter was healed. |

Making Connections

We use Matthew's version of this story, rather than Mark's, because it gives a clearer role for the Disciples. But Mark's version, the one that was written down earlier, makes it clear that Jesus' reason for this journey into foreign parts was that he wanted a holiday. It was a way of getting away from it all. Some hope!

No sooner is he away from the office than someone comes knocking on the door. Mark (7:24–30) tells us explicitly that the woman is a Greek, a Gentile, and specifies her nationality as Syro-Phoenician. More vaguely, Matthew says that she is a Canaanite, a member of the inferior pagan ethnic group that was, long ago, driven out from the Promised Land to make room for the Israelites. Both Evangelists make it clear that she is a Gentile mother; and, as so often with this sort of claimant, she wants Jesus' help on behalf of someone else. She comes as a complete outsider to the community of faith. She is not necessarily a poor person, financially. The Tyre and Sidon area is prosperous; Galilee depends on it as an export market; there are bigger profits to be made by selling bread in Tyre than back home in Galilee, and that causes some resentment. There could be quite a bit of complaint that honest Jews should not be delivering bread to these pagans.[1]

As a native of that area, the woman probably speaks to Jesus in Greek, and requires him to respond in a language that is not the easiest for him. She comes crying and wailing, calling on Jesus in terms of his religious and racial status. Jesus has brought his Disciples – his trainees, or students – with him on his short break. He cannot simply be at people's beck and call all the time. They have their agenda for this couple of days, and a foreign woman with her crazy demands is no part of it. The Disciples are highly embarrassed by this display, and suggest that he simply shoos her away. He is unwilling to take such a drastic step. But for as long as she shouts and bawls, emphasizing all the distances between himself and herself, he cannot communicate with her. In the face of her grovelling self-humiliation, he is silent.

But this cannot go on indefinitely. If it is wrong to send her away, he must do something to shift her out of her present state of mind; she is seeing him merely as a foreign magician of superior status, and that is exactly the opposite to genuine faith. So he speaks to her in the most discouraging way possible: 'It is wrong to take bread from the children and give it to the dogs.' Strictly, he uses a word meaning 'little dogs', which is possible in Greek but, apparently, not in Aramaic. Whatever the language, nothing can disguise the fact that Jesus speaks to her in a grossly insulting way.

What are her options? She has been stressing the difference between Jesus and herself, in the hope that, by flattery and by appeal to his status-consciousness, she can get what she wants. And it has not worked. So what is she to do now? She could make an even more pitiful appeal to the magic authority-figure. Or, she could curse him and stomp off, with a tale to tell about these snooty and hardhearted Jews. She discovers a third way. She realizes that although Jesus is a man, a Jew and Messiah into the bargain, she can argue back and put him right. She answers, 'Don't make too much of the difference between children and dogs; they get the same diet; they have the same needs, the same menu.' And Jesus has to acknowledge that she is right.

Before the daughter can be healed of her sickness, the mother has to be healed of her superstitious approach to authority and her exaggerated idea of the importance of human differences of status. And this involves pain and delay. It causes Jesus to display what looks like an uncharacteristic callousness. But, by this procedure, Jesus uncovers faith. He liberates the mother to announce a discovery that is a great surprise to Jesus himself.

The woman has no theological qualifications. She is uninstructed concerning the right ways of belief and conduct. But she has faith; and faith insists on refusing to be discouraged, even by one who has all the correct status. She hears Jesus saying that there is indeed bread for children; as a mother she knows that her daughter is entitled to a share with other children. A woman who fights for her suffering child protests against all that would tolerate that suffering. If the Son of David says that her daughter must just go on suffering, the Son of David must be wrong.

When Jesus comments on someone's faith, he is usually expressing surprise. 'What a lot I have to learn from you.' This unnamed alien woman is the clearest example in the Gospels of someone who teaches Jesus a lesson. He has to acknowledge that she is right: the distinction that he has tried to make between children and dogs just won't do. Jesus is not the one who knows everything in advance and who therefore has nothing to learn. As Son of God, he is the incarnation of the God who has created the universe and is constantly discovering how it works and how its potential is to be realized. Jesus is the learner, and discloses God who is a learner. Jesus is being educated by the woman; his boundaries are being enlarged, his attitudes shifted, by a nameless pagan who, for his Disciples, was just an irritating nuisance. And all this happens, characteristically, out on the frontier, well away from the formal institutions of holiness and the symbols of defined faith.

The early Christian communities had to learn the same lesson – sometimes, no doubt, by the hard way. Truth does not flow neatly from those who have got it to those who haven't. The gospel is a living power, not a commodity that can be distributed by those who control it. It happens in meetings out on the frontier, where there are few landmarks, where the Church and its ministers are unprotected, where they have no power or security, and where they do not have all the answers. The story is treasured by the Church because it helps us to make sense of this sort of thing as it happens to us.

We are the Body of Christ. A body is the person, acting, speaking, experiencing and being experienced by others. The Gospel story tells us what sort of things happened to the Christ incarnate. The same sort of things go on happening in the Body of Christ in the here-and-now.

As we meet at the Table of the Lord, we take the bread that was made available to this strange woman, with her tendency to shout and bawl, but also her quick wit. She is there before us, in the procession to Communion. We also are dogs, 'not worthy to gather up the crumbs under the Lord's table'. But whereas she comes to Jesus with a prayer of holy defiance, our liturgical piety gives us the self-suppression of the Prayer of Humble Access. If we would take her as a model for our approach to the Table of God, we ought to make a prayer that insists on our right to be there, because Christ has told us that there is bread for children; we ought to make a prayer of protest, rejecting all the conventions that get in the way of access for all the children of God to the things of God. The latest Church of England *Common Worship* book moves this prayer – which claims this woman as our model – from its previous fairly sensible position before the commencement of the Liturgy of the Sacrament, and tells us to offer it as our immediate response to the invitation 'Draw near with faith'. If we are indeed drawing near with faith, that faith should surely be something more like the bold faith of that woman, not a coy self-devaluing which says, in effect, 'Yes, all right, but I really oughtn't to'. And, to add to the irony, this is happening in a form of worship in which there is, normally, no bread for children!

For Working Groups

Ignition

What have you learned in the last week or last year or since Christmas? Who have you learned from?

Exploration

The group leader should give just enough information about the racial and social character of the woman, but otherwise let the story speak for itself.

Break into four teams:

1 Jesus
2 The woman
3 The Disciples
4 Matthew, our story-teller

Questions for Jesus, the
woman and the Disciples: *What are you doing here? What are your motives? What problems do you face? Who causes these problems? As the meeting between Jesus and the woman*

proceeds, what are
the options for you?
What ways out of the
situation are
possible? Why do you
react as you do?

Questions for Matthew: *Why do you bother
with this story, since
you may think it does
not show Jesus in a
very favourable light?
What use is it going
to be to your church?*

After a few minutes, each of the first three teams
chooses one or two members to go and visit another
team. The opening question for all visitors is: *In what
ways am I / are we a problem or a difficulty or a puzzle to
you?*

· Members from the Disciples team visit Jesus.
· Members from the woman team visit the Disciples.
· Members from the Jesus team visit the woman.
· The Matthew team splits up and goes to overhear the
  conversations between the other teams.

When this phase has gone on long enough, the visitors
return to their original teams, and the Matthew team
re-groups. The Matthew team can start the last phase
of this part of the meeting by giving its answers to the
questions that it has been considering.

Destination

Look at the last paragraph of the Exploration section. How far is your church learning? Who from?

Each member of your group is on some frontier or other. At some point, you are on the edge of the Christian community – or beyond the edge. You are alone, sent into a foreign scene where strange things happen, strange misunderstandings about Jesus or the Church are expressed, and strange people make sudden demands. You are not there by accident. You are there because God scatters the community that he gathers. Your presence out there is Christ's presence; your ministry is Christ's ministry. And things do not normally go according to plan.

What opportunities are there for those of you who live and work out on a frontier of some sort, to bring back what you experience and share it with the rest of us? What misunderstandings have you had to face? How do you respond – with irritation, jokes, correction, tolerance, or what?

How do you think we should take the Canaanite woman's words into our own prayer?

11

The Lady with the Hair

The Gospel Story

Luke 7:36–50

Narrator	A Pharisee invited Jesus to have dinner with him, and Jesus went to his house and sat down to eat. In that town was a woman who lived a sinful life. She heard that Jesus was eating in the Pharisee's house, so she brought an alabaster jar full of perfume and stood behind Jesus, by his feet, crying and wetting his feet with her tears. Then she dried his feet with her hair, kissed them, and poured the perfume on them. When the Pharisee saw this, he said to himself:
Simon	If this man really were a prophet, he would know who this woman is who is touching him; he would know what kind of sinful life she lives!
Narrator	Jesus spoke up and said to him:
Jesus	Simon, I have something to tell you.
Simon	Yes, Teacher, tell me.
Jesus	There were two men who owed money to a moneylender. One owed him five hundred silver coins, and the other owed

	him fifty. Neither of them could pay him back, so he cancelled the debts of both. Which one, then, will love him more?
Simon	I suppose that it would be the one who was forgiven more.
Jesus	You are right.
Narrator	Then he turned to the woman, and said to Simon:
Jesus	Do you see this woman? I came into your home, and you gave me no water for my feet, but she has washed my feet with her tears and dried them with her hair. You did not welcome me with a kiss, but she has not stopped kissing my feet since I came. You provided no olive-oil for my head, but she has covered my feet with perfume. I tell you, then, the great love she has shown proves that her many sins have been forgiven. But whoever has been forgiven little shows only a little love.
Narrator	Then Jesus said to the woman:
Jesus	Your sins are forgiven.
Narrator	The others sitting at the table began to say to themselves:
Person 1	Who is this?
Person 2	He even forgives sins?
Narrator	But Jesus said to the woman:
Jesus	Your faith has saved you; go in peace.

Making Connnections

A Deaf man, together with a sign-language interpreter, went for an appointment with a psychiatrist, and we accompanied them. At the end of a long conversation, the psychiatrist started to suggest some ideas for a diagnosis of the Deaf man's problems. He noted, as one of the symptoms, that the man had never looked at the psychiatrist during the conversation, and had not made any eye-contact with him. He felt that this body-language was very significant. We had to point out, as gently as we could, that the Deaf man was, rightly, engaged 100 per cent in watching the interpreter, and therefore couldn't be expected to watch the psychiatrist; and that, if he had looked at the psychiatrist's face at all, it would have been to watch his lips rather than his eyes. As it happened, the psychiatrist had a heavy beard, so there would not have been much point in even trying to read his lips! In spite of all this, however, the interview as a whole was helpful and productive.

There is, rightly, a lot of interest in body-language in these days. But some books suggest that reading body-language is as simple as 'the cat sat on the mat'. It is, in fact, marvellously easy to come to totally incorrect conclusions as we try to interpret body-language. In our home, we don't seem to get much better as the years go by!

In Luke's story, we have a dramatic and vigorous piece of body-language, with two wildly different interpretations. For Simon, the Pharisee, the activities of the woman were just part of her known character: she was a dangerous and dissolute person who could be guaranteed to try to seduce any man she could get within spitting-distance. So, any man with a scrap of discretion or morality would give her the brush-off as quickly as he could. Jesus must be a bogus prophet if he could not see this. He had brought Jesus to his house in no friendly or hospitable manner, in order to confirm his opinion that Jesus was a charlatan and ought to be exposed.

Simon suspects that Jesus cannot be a prophet because he cannot see into the woman's character. But Jesus demonstrates that he can detect Simon's inner thoughts. He responds to Simon with a simple parable, which tells him: you don't show much love because you don't have much to forgive. The woman shows a lot of love, and this shows that she has had a lot to forgive – and the forgiving has happened. Simon is a perfectly good person. Good luck to him. But he will never be much of a lover. The woman has been a bad person, but we are not told in what way; the traditional interpretation is that she has been a prostitute, and this may well be correct, because this was one of the few ways in which a woman had real opportunity to be visibly bad. The parable is given in economic terms, because one of the commonest understandings of sin is that sin is a debt owing to God. This is made explicit at the heart of the Lord's Prayer. In Luke's version, we ask that we may be released from the indebtedness of our offences against God, just as we release (same word) from debt those who are indebted to ourselves (Luke 11:4). Simon would be unwilling for the woman to be released from her indebtedness. Jesus says that this has already happened. Simon knows what she has been; Jesus can recognize what she has become. Simon sees the stereotype of 'prostitute'. Jesus sees an individual person, a person relating to God. Jesus is convinced; he has felt her hair stroking his feet, he smells the perfume; and his heart is touched by the tears with which all this is accompanied. He reads her body-language in a way that is totally different from Simon's. He sees it as evidence of the fact that she is already a forgiven person.

In the past, the woman has had the role of being on the receiving end of men's sexual demands. It is her job to respond, and to satisfy her customer's requirements. She also carries the burden of being labelled a 'sinner' – the guilt is attached to her, which would more properly be attached to her clients. They cause her role to exist. She has been using her female sexual identity to earn a living. Now, in her attention to Jesus, she is no less a woman than before. Only a person who is conscious and confident in her femininity could behave as she does. But now she is the one who takes the initiative. She is free. She is no longer a victim of the sexual system or the economic system or anything else. She is a released person – and the same word, in Greek and Hebrew, underlies the idea both of release and of forgiveness.

Jesus does not indicate when or how the woman has been forgiven. His point is that her behaviour is evidence of her forgiven-ness. When he eventually says, 'Your sins are forgiven', the literal meaning is, 'Your sins have been forgiven and remain forgiven'. Forgiven-ness is your character, your insignia, the environment that you carry around with you. This is salvation. Jesus does not claim to have saved her. Your faith has saved you. You take responsibility for what has happened to you. It is something in yourself that has brought about a change, which has released a generosity that is beyond the comprehension of the dull good man Simon.

People of Simon's type do not expect or want change. They feel secure when they see their stereotypes fulfilled. They treasure the Law; but they turn it from being an expression of God's justice and compassion into a way of keeping the unforgiven unforgiven, the poor poor, and the powerless powerless. What Jesus has done is to provide an environment within which the woman has been released and fulfilled. He has come bringing the release promised in the vision of Jubilee. The woman's reinstatement does not require elaborate and expensive rituals and sacrifices. Jesus has the authority to announce her reinstatement. She belongs within the peace – the *shalom* – of God. Whatever may have been her past, this is her present. And it is her future. Luke uses the Greek language carefully: according to his story, Jesus' final word to the woman is 'Go *into* peace, the *shalom* which is ahead of you'.

All our Churches, whatever their tradition, know that they have a responsibility to represent Christ's mission of forgiveness. Most Churches ordain their ministers with some sort of commitment to be responsible agents of this forgiveness. This is made very clear in the Christian tradition to which I myself belong, and it worries me that so rarely do our Churches and ministers specifically advertise that they are in the business of making God's grace of absolution available. But the question still remains: do we accept each other, in the Christian fellowship, as people who have received absolution? One of the most ecumenical features of the Churches, right across the spectrum of Christian tradition, is our capacity for censoriousness. We still believe that a person's guilt is an essential part of their identity, especially if the guilt is something conspicuous or criminal. And it is quite possible for a person to make a sincere confession of sin, and to receive absolution, but still to be treated by other Christians as a guilty person. Clergy who hear confessions know this. Some discharged prisoners know it more painfully.

So what is the point of our repeated 'general confessions' – the formula repeated Sunday by Sunday by the whole congregation, usually fairly early in the course of our worship? It is always possible for a group of people, who are charitable and humble as individuals, to form an exclusive, proud and censorious community, eager to detect faults and to compare themselves favourably with the dissolute world around them. The intention of our confession is to express the sense that we are attracted into the worshipping fellowship by the message that our God is a God of forgiveness. If this is truly so, the forgiven community will willingly accept the forgiven individual.

The gospel announces to us that only the forgiving can be forgiven; but also only the forgiven can forgive. This would place us in an insoluble dilemma, if it were not that Christ comes into our world first, making forgiveness available before we know we need it. In this way, the congregation itself becomes a community of absolution, a community of priests. Our gathering is a celebration of Christ's company with the undeserving. We break bread together, and can

afford to be uninterested in whether anyone qualifies or
not. We meet to celebrate God's intention of cancelling
indebtedness, and of banishing compassionlessness from
creation.

For Working Groups

This is probably not a story for a large group, or for a
new group of people who do not know and trust each
other. There is a lot of emotion and, perhaps, pain that
may emerge to be exposed as we get into the experiences of the characters. Some members may have memories that get awakened, memories of embarrassment
or of shame. Jesus did not keep himself distant from
prostitutes, or from men who might have used prostitutes; there is surely no reason why this should not also
be true of our Church groups. Jesus was gentle but firm
with Simon; it was an embarrassing situation, but it
did take place in a domestic situation, not in the middle
of a crowd of strangers. A working group of people who
trust each other should be able to gain much from a
careful reflection on the story.

Ignition

Would two people be willing to offer, in advance, to take
on and mime the roles of the woman and Jesus? There
is no need for a lengthy re-enactment. But the woman
should have hair long enough to be able to stroke the
man's feet with it, as he reclines at a table. This is a
story with a lot of experience of touching, and we would
miss out on the feel and meaning of it if we stay with
mere talking.

Exploration

Three small teams, in twos or threes, can spend a few
minutes thinking themselves into the experience of
Simon, the woman and Jesus. They can then come
together. They can imagine what it would be like for
the three participants to meet again, a few weeks after
the event recorded by Luke. They can compare their
memories of what took place.

Destination

Do we, as a Church, behave as a group of people who
are genuinely forgiven?

12

Bending the Mind of the Lawyer

The Gospel Story

Luke 10:25–37

Narrator	A teacher of the Law came up and tried to trap Jesus.
Lawyer	Teacher, what must I do to receive eternal life?
Narrator	Jesus answered him:
Jesus	What do the Scriptures say? How do you interpret them?
Lawyer	'Love the Lord your God with all your heart, with all your soul, with all your strength, and with all your mind'; and 'Love your neighbour as you love yourself.'
Jesus	You are right; do this and you will live.
Narrator	But the teacher of the Law wanted to justify himself, so he asked Jesus:
Lawyer	Who is my neighbour?
Jesus	There was once a man who was going down from Jerusalem to Jericho when robbers attacked him, stripped him, and beat him up, leaving him half dead. It so happened that a priest was going down that road; but when he saw the man, he

walked on by, on the other side. In the same way a Levite also came along, went over and looked at the man, and then walked on by, on the other side. But a Samaritan who was travelling that way came upon the man, and when he saw him, his heart was filled with pity. He went over to him, poured oil and wine on his wounds and bandaged them; then he put the man on his own animal and took him to an inn, where he took care of him. The next day he took out two silver coins and gave them to the innkeeper.

Samaritan   Take care of him, and when I come back this way, I will pay you whatever else you spend on him.

Narrator   And Jesus concluded:

Jesus   In your opinion, which one of these three acted like a neighbour towards the man attacked by the robbers?

Narrator   The teacher of the Law answered:

Lawyer   The one who was kind to him.

Jesus   You go, then, and do the same.

Making Connections

Here we have another story of a journey. This time, however, it is not a journey that can be worked out on a map. It is a process that could be represented completely by two talking heads. But it is a journey nevertheless – a journey of experiment and discovery.

Luke gives us a story within a story. We will miss the point of the parable if we do not recognize the story within which it is set. The story of the priest, the Levite and the Samaritan should not be detached from its context: the story of Jesus and the lawyer. The whole story is a story of healing and salvation, just as much as, for instance, the stories of Zacchaeus and of Bartimaeus.

The lawyer presents a problem to Jesus, and Jesus uses the parable as an instrument for responding to the problem. We can get into the story by trying to feel what is happening to the lawyer, and by seeing how Jesus faces the problem.

The lawyer has a question: this isn't the problem itself, but it is the first part of the problem. Jesus refuses to act as an authority: he pushes the question back to the lawyer. The lawyer produces the right answer; he quotes a combination of texts that elsewhere in the Gospels has the authority of Jesus himself. So Jesus affirms that the lawyer can, within the tools and resources of his profession and his tradition, discover the answers. He does not need Jesus to tell him what God primarily requires. Indeed, when people tell us that Jesus came to tell us to love each other, they are really saying that he was redundant; we do not need to have the Son of God incarnated to tell us to love each other; we can get all that from Moses. So, let the lawyer make the most of what he has already got.

The lawyer then tries, reasonably enough, to get a clearer definition. What is the use of a law if its terms aren't clear? Please provide a definition of 'neighbour'. The problem for Jesus now arises. What are his options? Should he give a straight authoritative answer? This would confirm the lawyer in his belief that definitions will solve the root problem. Should he rebuke the lawyer for asking the wrong question? This would destroy the basis of confidence that has been built up so far. So Jesus tells the parable.

Who would the lawyer identify with? In terms of profession and culture, it would be with the priest and Levite. They would naturally be his neighbours. He might well grieve for their failure to comply with the good precepts of compassion, but he would know priests and Levites personally, and would excuse them on the grounds that touching a dead or apparently dead body would make them ritually unclean and therefore would disable them from their roles in the system of purity, on which the culture of the nation depended. It could disqualify them for life. But the lawyer would not have any Samaritan friends. He would know only the stereotype of the Samaritan. For the lawyer, a 'good Samaritan' would be a contradiction in terms, like a Swiss battleship. Samaritan-ness was a moral category; it designated a people of inferior quality by definition. Samaritans were really the lowest of the low. They were worse than the Roman colonialists, because, in their schismatic and heretical ways, they were a continual reminder to Jews of the danger of unfaithfulness. They were the enemy in the midst.

As a response to the question, Jesus' parable does not fit. To provide an answer to the question, 'Who is my neighbour?' the story *ought* to be about a wise person surveying three different people and deciding which of them qualified to be recognized as neighbour and which did not. That kind of story would fit the lawyer's question. But Jesus turns the question inside out and tells a story of these three people's different courses of action. Two of the people do not behave as neighbours. The third does so, and the details are spelled out; he carefully applies cleansing and disinfecting agents – oil and wine – at the same time as he does the bandaging. He forgoes the use of his own transport by putting the wounded man on his animal, and he commits himself unreservedly to financial support. In the end the question is no longer 'Who qualifies to be called neighbour?' but 'Who has behaved as a neighbour?' Strictly speaking, the question is, 'Which of them *became* a neighbour?' The third man did not have neighbourliness as a qualification or status; a neighbour is something that we become, through our neighbourly action. Literally, the lawyer replies, 'He that *did* mercy.' So, the neighbour is not the other person: the neighbour is you, if you behave in a neighbourly way. If you don't behave as a neighbour, don't say that it's because of something about the other person – some disqualification in terms of age or sex or race or character; if you don't act as a neighbour, the reason is in yourself. In the form of a theory, this is a difficult distinction to put into words: even a lawyer might have problems with it. In the form of a story, the distinction jumps into light; you can see the point if you allow yourself to see it.

It is important for us to recognize the difficulty of the question that Jesus is asking. I have heard several modern versions of the story. Most of them have been all right in principle, but not particularly shocking. But there is one version that has stayed with me. It told of a little old lady being mugged in a tube-train, and three people coming to look at her. The first two, who moved away in their professional self-concern, were a vicar and a social worker – predictably. The third, who did all the necessary things, of gentle care and generous support, was a foul-mouthed football hooligan, straight from a street battle. And I found myself protesting, 'This is over the top! It's absurd; a football hooligan could not possibly act like that!' Exactly! As a vicar myself, I knew plenty of vicars and social workers, and I knew that we could indeed act like our representatives in the story. But a football hooligan? In my little world, I had no friends who were football hooligans. I knew such characters only as a stereotype, as the lawyer would know Samaritans as a stereotype. And the stereotype makes the real person incredible. Unless you feel the force of a similar protest in the mind of the lawyer, you haven't caught the sharp edge of Jesus' story. A Samaritan! Impossible! A Samaritan just could not possibly act like that!

Can the lawyer allow himself to identify with the Samaritan? He has the integrity to see that the Samaritan is the neighbourly person. And the reason for this is not necessarily that the Samaritan is better than the priest and the Levite, but that he is more free. He is not inhibited by the claims of religious duty and dangers of ritual uncleanness. He is not too busy: he has less to lose. The status of priest and Levite makes it more difficult for them to be neighbours. So, therefore, does the status of lawyer. But there is hope for the lawyer. He shows that he can transcend his own professional and religious identity: he can acknowledge which of the three was the neighbour. He can see that the commitment to the laws of purity of the professional people of religion – including himself – is no guarantee that they will obey the fundamental law of charity, or that they will represent God's purpose of setting his people free.

Jesus sets the lawyer free. He provides a real-life situation to give the lawyer the opportunity to look at his own preconceptions. He achieves a miracle of salvation with this lawyer. He enables the lawyer to discover that he can be more than a lawyer, just as the Samaritan is more than a Samaritan. But the lawyer remains a lawyer; it is in the integrity of his profession that he is able to acknowledge that it was the Samaritan who acted as neighbour, and therefore fulfilled the law of charity, and not the others. So Jesus can reasonably say to him, 'Go and do as he did'. Go and take the Samaritan as your example. Defy the expectations of professional people. Join Jesus, and take the journey downwards. You can do it: you don't have to be limited by your privilege, your education, your religion: above all, you don't have to be limited by your moral status, your goodness. You have the potential to be a neighbour, and nothing in your status can stand in your way. Even you can become a neighbour, just as the Samaritan became a neighbour.

Jesus never demands the impossible. He is not in business to maximize guilt by telling people to do things that they cannot do. But he knows that people can do a whole lot more than they think they can do. He does not stay with the actuality, he pushes us into our potential, beyond our expectation. Go and have a shot at it yourself.

This is gospel for the privileged; even the members of the

conventional establishment of the day can join the community of mercy. There is an ancient cynical question, 'Can Archdeacons be saved?' Here is an answer. It is just possible – by a miracle – for an ecclesiastical official to achieve truth and salvation. To those of us who are, in one way or another, officials of a religious system, the message is: you do have some disadvantages when it comes to fulfilling God's will, but it is not impossible for you to do so, provided that you let go of your reliance on your religious role. But don't be surprised if people who care little for your religious standards get there ahead of you!

By the time that Luke told the story the situation had already changed. Samaritans and other religiously second-class people were already dominant in the Church. The new Christian communities were full of non-entities (1 Corinthians 1:26–29). They would have the problem the other way round: for them, perhaps, the biting point in the story would be not that the Samaritan is the neighbourly person to identify with but that the Jewish lawyer can find his way into the community of neighbourliness. Perhaps, over the centuries, the Gentiles have shown themselves less willing than the lawyer to recognize that Jews and non-Jews can be in a community of mutual trust, honouring and service.

We often use this story as an example of compassion. This is not wrong, but it misses the main point. The key issue in the story as a whole is how Jesus educates the lawyer. It is a wonderful example of how people can be gently led into discovering much more truth about themselves than they could ever have expected.

Jesus' teaching is a response to a genuine question; it is not part of a syllabus that he has himself devised. The good educator is not in control of the agenda; he does not know all the subjects in advance.

Jesus does not give a direct answer to the lawyer. He throws the lawyer back on his own resources. The lawyer can actually answer his own questions; his presenting of a question, therefore, is not to gain further knowledge but to 'justify himself' – to establish his own credential as a legal mind. The parable is not given as a 'sermon-illustration', an imaginative device to drive home a general point already being made, or to brighten up a dull talk; rather, it is given as a way of giving the hearer a chance to decide whether to hear or whether to refuse to hear. It throws the responsibility on to the hearer, so that the hearers' responses are genuinely their own and are not just a feeding-back of what has been given to them. So this is a characteristic parable; it sets the hearers free to take responsibility for their own responses.

By telling this sort of story, Jesus invites the lawyer – and his other listeners who might have been overhearing – to identify with one or other of the characters. The lawyer would naturally start by identifying with the priest and the Levite. In our studies of Gospel stories, we are using these stories in much the same way. We are being asked to identify with the roles and persons within the narratives, and to see where they lead us.

This is the classic example of Jesus as the bringer of salvation by his teaching. But, did he really teach? Oscar Wilde is near to the truth when he says that Christ is like a work of art. 'He does not really teach one anything, but by being brought into his presence one becomes something'.[1] This could be a much better model for the Church's teaching role than any catechism, in which the teacher knows all the answers in advance.

For Working Groups

Ignition

What have you been learning in the last week (or year)?
Who have you been learning from? How?

   Let members think about this, and share with each
other in twos or threes, for a few minutes.

Exploration

Break into five teams:

1 The priest/Levite
2 The Samaritan
3 The lawyer
4 Jesus
5 Luke, our story-teller

Questions for the priest/Levite and the Samaritan:	*What sort of person am I? Why do I behave as I do?*
Questions for the lawyer:	*What do you want when you approach Jesus? What happens to you in the course of the story?*
Questions for Jesus:	*What is the problem that the lawyer's approach presents to you? Why do you*

Questions for Luke: *respond in the way you do? Why do you record this story? How do you think it will be understood by the Church for which you are writing?*

The teams take between six and ten minutes to work at these questions. Then the first four teams each choose one or two members to visit other teams.

- Members from the Jesus team visit the Samaritan, and ask: *Why do you think I put you in the story?*
- Members from the Samaritan team visit the priest/Levite, and ask: *Why do you and I behave so differently from each other?*
- Members from the priest/Levite team visit the lawyer, and ask: *What is your opinion of us and our behaviour?*
- Members from the lawyer team visit Jesus, and ask: *Why do you answer me in the way you do?*
- The Luke team splits up and goes to overhear the conversations between the other teams.

When the four conversations have gone on for long enough, the teams re-assemble. Then the Luke team can start off a plenary discussion, by offering answers to the questions that it has been dealing with.

Destination

How is education happening in our church? How far are
we able to learn from each other? What opportunities
are there for genuine and careful sharing of experience? What experiences have we had that could teach
us in the same way as we are taught by the parables of
Jesus?

13

The Opening Programme

The Gospel Story

Mark 7:31–37

Narrator	Jesus left the neighbourhood of Tyre and went on through Sidon to Lake Galilee, going by way of the territory of the Ten Towns. Some people brought him a man who was deaf and could hardly speak, and they begged Jesus to place his hands on him. So Jesus took him off alone, away from the crowd, put his fingers in the man's ears, spat and touched the man's tongue. Then Jesus looked up to heaven, gave a deep groan, and said to the man:
Jesus	Ephphatha! Open up!
Narrator	At once the man was able to hear, his speech impediment was removed, and he began to talk without any trouble. Then Jesus ordered the people not to speak of it to anyone; but the more he ordered them not to, the more they spoke. And all who heard were completely amazed.
Person 1	How well he does everything! He even causes the deaf to hear and the dumb to speak!

Making Connections

Centuries before Christ, people were saying, 'What a wonderful thing it will be when the blind can see, and the deaf hear, when the cripples can join the dance and the stammerers join the choir. What a wonderful day it will be when the Lord comes to us to make all this possible!' (Isaiah 35:5–6).

This is the hope that Jesus comes to fulfil. He comes opening people's eyes and ears, their minds and lives. He travels around the country, meeting all sorts of different people. In chs. 7 and 8, Mark describes him taking a strange wandering route; if taken literally on the map, it is a real dog's hind leg of a trip. But one point is very clear: each of the places mentioned is on a frontier, far away from the respectable centres of society and of holiness. Isaiah's prophecy tells of a new status and future for disabled people, and also for despised and useless places. This is all part of God's 'vengeance', his setting right of the inequalities and disadvantages of the world.

On this journey, a man is brought to Jesus who is inevitably a target for his interest, a closed man, a man who is Deaf and who has therefore been unable to learn how to speak fluently. Mark uses a very unusual word to describe this man with his speech-problem – *mogilalos* (stammerer). The man was not 'dumb'; Deaf people very rarely are. Some people still ignorantly use the phrase 'deaf and dumb', but this is misleading. The reason why Deaf people sometimes speak differently from hearing people is that they have not been able to learn to speak by hearing. So their speech sounds 'abnormal', and 'stammering' may be a reasonable word to use to describe it. But Mark does not often use unusual terms – he usually keeps to a fairly simple vocabulary. There is only one other place in the whole Bible in Greek where this word is used – in the prophecy of Isaiah, which I have already quoted. So Mark is saying that in Jesus this prophecy is being fulfilled. Jesus is bringing this 'day of vengeance'. The future has become present; disabilities and prejudices are being overcome, barriers are being knocked away, out there in the borderlands.

Here is a group of people who realize that a new possibility is present. They bring their Deaf friend to Jesus. Jesus deals with this man with remarkable precision. He does what few hearing people do: he communicates with the Deaf person on the Deaf person's own terms. This is empathy. He evidently says to himself, 'What is it like to be this man?' He recognizes the culture and communication-methods of the Deaf person; he does not try to force him to be like a hearing person. 'When I empathize with you, I leave where I am and go to be with you where you are.'

Such a man cannot be dealt with as just a member of a crowd: there is no point in putting him in a congregation and hoping that he will get what he needs from a general sermon addressed to people at large. He will not hear. He, as a Deaf man, is used to being ignored by people around him: he is used to seeing people in conversation and having no share in their fellowship. Unless it is made very clear to him that a communication is for him, he will assume that it is for someone else. This is part of his closedness: this is what society is doing to him.

So Jesus deals with this man absolutely personally: he takes him away from the distractions and interferences of the crowd. He makes it absolutely clear that he is communicating with the Deaf man and with nobody else. He realizes that the Deaf man will judge him by the way he looks and the things he does, rather than by what he says. He knows that the man depends on his sight and touch-perception rather than on his hearing, so he makes the fullest possible use of these senses. He does not shout and make the man feel stupid. He does not try to make the man do what he *cannot* do; he makes the best use of what the man *can* do. He communicates to the man what he intends to do with signs that could not be improved upon by any modern expert in sign-language. He uses very precise sacramental signs, not just the generalized 'laying on of hands' that the friends asked for. He draws the man into a conspiracy of healing. He doesn't just 'work a miracle' impersonally; he involves the man in the process. This is not just 'spiritual' healing; it is sacramental, incarnational, touching the flesh, sharing physical spit, using all the available sensory systems.

Jesus communicates in a way that tells the Deaf man that the language of Deaf people is an honourable way of communicating, a language fit for the Son of God. He loves the Deaf people; you cannot love people if you do not take their language seriously. In sign-language, Jesus tells the man that he will hear, and will be able to speak clearly. He lifts his eyes to heaven, to show that the healing will come from God, not by the personal magic of Jesus. He sighs, to indicate that the new creation will come through the power of the Holy Spirit. Jesus does not confuse the man with lots of words, but he does use one word, a word so significant that Mark records it for us in the original Aramaic which Jesus spoke: '*Ephphatha*', 'be opened'. For the most part, we do not know what Jesus actually said; his home-language was Aramaic, but we normally hear his voice only through the filters and distortions involved in the process of translation into Greek – and then, of course, through the further filters and distortions involved in the process of translation into English. But occasionally we do hear the actual sounds that he made. And here we have an example. We can tell from the translation, 'be opened', that it is a very meaningful word that Jesus uses; but only because Mark gives us the Aramaic original can we see that Jesus selects a word that is exceptionally easy to lip-read. The Greek equivalent *dianoichtheti* would be difficult – the lip-movements for D, N, and T are indistinguishable. The English version 'be opened' is almost impossible – B and P look identical.

Ephphatha is a gift to the lip-reader. Jesus evidently has the instinct to choose this particular word; the medium precisely fits the message. And, although we have no reason to believe that Mark had any specialist knowledge of deafness, he has had the insight to share these details with us.

The word *Ephphatha* is not merely a mouthing; it does have a precise meaning. It is an attack on the man's closedness. So the man hears. Because he is able to hear, his speech becomes clear. And people realize that in Jesus the new age has appeared. As in the first creation, God in Christ is doing all things well. This is the new creation. We can see what he does and proclaim that it is good.

Deafness is classified as a disability. Like blindness and lameness, it is a condition where the person is missing some ability that most people possess. It is a fact of life, and in many cases there is not a lot that can be done to correct the disability. But a handicap is something very different. A handicap is what society does with the disability. A person may have no use of her legs; that is a disability. Its effect can be reduced if she is provided with a wheelchair. But if she is faced with a building that has a long flight of steps at the entrance, the disability becomes a handicap. She is prevented from having access to a facility to which most people have access. Deafness is a disability. If society devalues the Deaf person's natural language, rubbishes it and refuses to allow it any status in education and law, then that ensures that deafness is also a handicap. This story of Jesus has inspired many enterprises in the attempt to prevent the disability from being a handicap. Schools that take seriously the natural communication-systems of Deaf people have been ways in which Christ continues to say the word *Ephphatha* – the word that opens people to communication. This is not just a matter of talking. It is a matter of overcoming the effects of deafness. Deafness isolates. The Deaf person is very often left out of any conversation.

Hearing people are frequently impatient. The old 'deaf-and-dumb' stereotype dies hard. Deaf people still find that they are treated as if they are stupid. Any sensible English-speaking hearing person will make allowances for the efforts of a German-speaking person to speak English; they will realize that, for the German, English is a second language. For many thousands of Deaf people in Britain, English is a second language; but the systems of law and education give little recognition to their first language, British Sign Language. After many years of struggle, the Welsh rightly have areas where their language has priority status, where it is legally recognized. Not so for the communicators in British Sign Language. But perhaps by the time that this book is published the movement for the recognition of British Sign Language will have had some success. If so, Deaf people will have gained some of the respect which, according to this story, Christ himself has accorded to them.[1]

The deaf people whom most hearing people will meet are, probably, 'deafened' – people who have become deaf in the course of their life, often in their later years. The loss of hearing is, of course, a grievous experience, and anything that can be done to ease the loss, by means of such things as loop systems, is wise and helpful. But such people have their memory of spoken language; the methods and structure of spoken language remain their basic way of understanding and communicating. People who have never really heard spoken language have a quite different way of understanding things. Their language is visual. It is people of this kind who are most severely excluded from the mainstream of society. Modern practice is to refer to such people as 'Deaf', and to refer to other people with hearing-loss as 'Deaf'. The practical dividing-line is often on the issue of whether the person concerned is able to use the telephone. It is with a Deaf man that Jesus communicates in this story. He affirms the Deaf person's way of communicating, and affirms the Deaf person's place within the healed community.

Jesus' home-language was Aramaic. He also would have had some schooling in Hebrew. He could converse with a Greek-speaking woman. And he communicated with a Deaf person. The Church is called to communicate in the languages that are natural to the people whom it serves. The Church in Wales, for instance, is a tri-lingual Church. But, in Church as well as in society as a whole, users of minority languages are not always recognized in their own right. I remember the struggle that we had for a Deaf ordination candidate to be given training and assessment procedures which were appropriate for him and which were not simply a pressurizing into conformity with the norms of a hearing system. Praise God for those structures, par-ticularly within the medium of TV, which have been treating the language of Deaf people with some degree of justice and honour.

For Working Groups

Ignition

Have you been in a situation where something was going on which you did not understand, when there was no way of finding out what was going on, where the words were in a foreign language – or perhaps in a foreign script which you could not even pronounce? What did it feel like?

Share your experience for a few minutes, in twos or threes. Try to empathize with someone who cannot hear. It's not enough to put ear-plugs in your ears, or to pretend to be deaf; you will still retain your hearing-person's way of understanding and using words. You

have to ask the empathy-question: What does it feel
like to be you?

Exploration

Read the story.

Break into four teams:

1 Jesus
2 The Deaf man
3 The friends
4 Mark, our story-teller

Questions for Jesus,
the Deaf man
and the friends: *What exactly is the
                              problem for you in
                              this situation?
                              What do you want?
                              What, in detail,
                              happens? Make a list
                              of the stages in the
                              process. What do you
                              see as the purpose of
                              each?*

Questions for Mark: *Why do you include
                              this story? How is it
                              going to be of value to
                              your readers?*

When the teams have had sufficient time to deal with
the questions, they can re-assemble as one group. They

should share their impressions of the sequence of events, and the purpose of each stage in the process. The Mark team should share its response to its questions.

Destination

Where does your local church fit into the experience of this story?

Is it the group of friends who bring the Deaf man to Jesus? Is it Christ's Body, working as Jesus worked? Is it really alongside people, using their language? Or does it expect people to adapt themselves to its language?

How far are you learning the skill of empathy, moving from where you are to where the other person is?

Does your church function in ways that are small enough to enable individuals to 'open up'? Do you have elements in your total programme that can enable this sort of closeness? Is your church like the praising crowd, noticing and celebrating the new creation that God is bringing in among you? How far are you on the watch for signs of God's creative presence in your world, bringing not only comfort but also justice; not only peace but also a restoration of lost dignity?

How far is your church involved in practical ways of assisting people with hearing-loss? For instance, have you consulted Deaf or Hard-of-Hearing people about the effectiveness of your church's sound-amplification system? Do you make effective use of the various visual elements of Christian communication – the essential visualness of the sacraments, the use of movement and picture and drama and diagrams on an overhead

projector? Anything that is good for children is likely to
be good for Deaf people, but this is on the understanding
that they are treated as spiritually and intellectually
adult and not as juveniles. Do you have a loop system?
Do you check similarly on this kind of provision in the
meeting-halls of your area, so that, for instance, Deaf
people are not excluded from political meetings?

Are you alert to the needs of Deaf and Hard-of-
Hearing people in your area who may need the specialist care of the Church's ministry with Deaf people? How
far are you in touch with organizations that are strug-
gling for the rights of Deaf people to have British Sign
Language given official recognition in the educational
and legal systems of this country – and in Europe?
There are issues here that should require your church
to make use of its personal links with your local council,
with your MP and MEP, and with the other govern-
mental institutions of the UK.

There is a considerable agenda that can arise from
what may appear to be a short and simple story!

14

The Ten Per Cent Return

The Gospel Story

Luke 17:11–19

Narrator	Now on his way to Jerusalem, Jesus travelled along the border between Samaria and Galilee. As he was going into a village, ten men who had leprosy met him. They stood at a distance and called out in a loud voice:
Man 1	Jesus!
Man 2	Master!
Man 1	Have pity on us!
Narrator	Jesus saw them.
Jesus	Go, show yourselves to the priests.
Narrator	And as they went they were cleansed. One of them, when he saw that he was healed, came back, praising God in a loud voice. He threw himself at Jesus' feet and thanked him – and he was a Samaritan. Jesus asked:
Jesus	Were not all ten cleansed? Where are the other nine? Was no one found to return and give glory to God except this foreigner?

Narrator	Then he said to him:
Jesus	Rise and go; your faith has saved you.

Making Connections

In the culture of the people of the Bible, leprosy was both a physical illness and a social disability. Physically, the disease was probably not the same as the disease that is called 'leprosy' today. But it was regarded with disgust and terror. There were rules of hygiene to isolate lepers, to protect society from the infection of this terrible skin disease. But leprosy was much more than a physical ailment; it was seen as a punishment for sin (e.g. 2 Chronicles 26:19). Everything combined to make lepers know that they were unacceptable, and to remind other people that it was a religious duty to make lepers feel unacceptable.

Perhaps this was not the original intention of the law. But it became the effect of the law. The law cannot heal; it can only protect. It cannot save; it can only encourage people to avoid the experiences and the contacts that may make them feel that they need to be saved. The law cannot make anyone acceptable; it can only give us the signs and guides to justify our unwillingness to accept each other.

The leper exists as an unclean person, compared with the rest of us who can feel that we are clean. The leper is the abnormal person, compared with the rest of us who can feel that we are normal. Society needs a supply of people who are unfit to share in society, so that the rest of us can feel all right. The successful majority need a failure-minority so that we may feel secure in our success.

It follows that it must be very difficult for anyone to move out of this role. The leper is needed by society; and society will not make it easy for the leper to cease to be a leper. For the people of the Bible, to be cured of leprosy was as difficult as to change the colour of one's skin; it was as difficult as raising the dead.

Jesus is not a stranger to the agonies of lepers. Early in his ministry, he has angrily defied the rules and touched a leper. His anger is not caused by the leper's approach or the danger of contamination, but by the whole system, which can so degrade a fellow human-being. His touch shows that he is willing to accept contamination; more eloquently than any words, it affirms that the leper is an acceptable and loveable person (Mark 1:40–45; Luke 5:12–14).

Now, later in the story, Jesus is with his disciples in a border-land. Galilee is an area far from the centre of holiness and religious orthodoxy in Jerusalem. Samaria is an area of religious alienation, the home of the half-breed community known as Samaritans. It is in this disordered area that Jesus meets a new demand. As so often, his work of healing and compassion happens on a frontier. In Jesus' story, holiness and salvation and contact with God do not happen first at the centre of power, to flow out to the edge. Jesus' work happens on the edge; and the task of his followers is to take an awareness of it to the so-called centre. We shall see this pattern working out more than once.

Jesus meets a whole group of outcast people. The leprosy makes them a community of disadvantage and exclusion. So Jesus deals with them not as separate individuals but as a group. He does not stop to check their credentials one by one. He recognizes their solidarity in rejectedness. They are disabled as a category; they are attended to as a category.

The lepers make a common song, a united claim, 'Lord, have mercy'. This is their chorus, 'Kyrie Eleison'. When the Church sings this song, it is taking on its lips the cry of all who are thus excluded and disabled.

The group of lepers keep the rules. They stay at a proper distance. Jesus is approaching the village from the north, and is preparing to enter it. The lepers cannot enter the village. So they face north and shout to Jesus across the valley. Jesus tells them to go to the Medical Officer of Health in the Temple at Jerusalem, where they can get a certificate of freedom from infection. This will qualify them to re-enter decent society. They take him at his word; they move off southwards, fulfilling the instructions that Jesus has given. As they travel in this direction, they discover that the marks of their disease have disappeared. The majority continue on their way to the office to get their certificates. But one of them finds that he cannot merely obey instructions; he detaches himself, turns completely round, runs across the divide, and comes right up to Jesus. He prostrates himself at Jesus' feet, and gives loud and glad thanks to God for his healing.

All ten have been healed of their disease. All ten have been 'cleansed' – their stigma of social unacceptability has been removed. But they are no longer ten. They have become nine and one. And the nine might reasonably ask, 'What's wrong with old Fred? Why can't he obey a simple order? Why can't we stick together? Why do we have to lose the friendship that we have made with each other during the bad times?'

But, for the one leper who turned back, the removal of the disadvantage shared with the other nine has disclosed a further level of disadvantage, a disadvantage not shared with the other nine. The tenth leper is a Samaritan.

The Samaritans were people who belonged nowhere. They were of the same original stock as the Jew, so they could not claim to be Gentile. But they were reckoned to be members of a degenerate offshoot of Judaism. The word translated 'foreigner' has religious as well as racial significance. Both religiously and racially, they were half-breeds; they were reminders to the Jews of their need to avoid further mistakes and compromises. In referring to this Samaritan, Jesus uses a word that was used in an inscription at the Temple entrance, warning 'Aliens, keep out'. Only if one had the appalling misfortune to be a leper could the difference between Jew and Samaritan be made more or less insignificant. Only as lepers could they call out in unison, 'Have mercy on *us*'.

In their disability as lepers, the ten are in solidarity with each other. But a solidarity in disadvantage means that we depend on the disadvantage. Healing brings division; take away the cause for complaint, and the unity is broken. That can be the effect of the ministry of Jesus.

The removal of the leprosy does make it reasonable to tell this Samaritan to go to the Temple and claim access to the priests for this particular purpose (this special privilege was apparently still available to Samaritans, but on any other occasion they would have no access to the Temple, because their religion was centred on the rival shrine at Mount Gerizim). But otherwise, the Samaritan is no more able to enter 'clean' society than when he was a leper. He would not be able to go with the others into public places of refreshment or entertainment or worship. For the other nine, their previous companion would now be an embarrassment. They would have good reason to be glad to see the back of him, and could proceed all the more speedily towards their destination at the office of the Medical Officer of Health.

This is an unusual story in the Gospels; it is one of the rare occasions where Jesus is described as healing people in a group or category. But it is an important story for any programme of study concerning 'salvation', because Luke – a skilled writer in Greek, who uses words with care and precision – specifically uses three distinct words to describe the therapy which happened to these lepers. Ten are 'healed' – they receive a cure for their physical ailment. Ten are 'cleansed' – they receive social acceptability. One is 'saved'; and this is a place where, I suggest, the conventional translation 'make well' or 'get well' is completely inadequate. The 'saved' person is the one who comes into personal contact with Christ. The 'saved' person is the one who joins in the community of thanksgiving, the community of 'Eucharist'. To be 'cleansed' and to be 'healed' mean that one is returning to a previous state of normality. To be 'saved' means that something quite new has happened.

Jesus does not totally disregard the regulations about purity that are managed by the priests. As with his previous encounter with a leper, he recognizes that these lepers have a right and a duty to avail themselves of the hygiene laws of society. Nine go their way to the Temple. But when the tenth comes to Jesus, he comes to one who is making the Temple redundant. A new Temple, and a new priesthood, are being offered to the diseased world.

Ten receive the blessings of healing and cleansing. The nine are not blamed or punished. Their blessing is not removed. Where Jesus is, the boundaries of disease and disorder are pushed back. But not everyone realizes what this means. Not everyone finds their way personally to Jesus. Only one in ten insists on going beyond the satisfaction of immediate needs, and comes to discover the source of the healing. He is the awkward ten per cent. If, in our involvement with such enterprises as schools and hospitals, we get only a ten per cent return in terms of any real commitment, we are doing all right – we are getting the same results as Jesus. If, out of the totality of your human nature, ten per cent of it is getting into something like a relationship with the divine, it may seem small, but there's good hope for you!

Of the one, Jesus says 'Your faith has saved you'. He does not insist that he, Jesus, has brought about the change. It is something in the Samaritan leper himself that has 'saved' him. Faith is an option for the one who suffers from a double disadvantage. Faith is the ability to recognize an alternative urgency. Faith is a willingness to take responsibility for oneself and not merely to do what one is told to do – even when the one who gives the instruction is Jesus. But Jesus provides the environment within which this faith can happen and have its saving effect.

Ten have good fortune; one has the faith that turns this good fortune into thankfulness, into the praise of God. This goes beyond the individual feelings. 'The praise of God is the re-creation of an unblemished world.'[1] The praise of God is the recognition of a new thing coming in; we are not merely being restored to a previous satisfactory status quo but are moving into a new creation. Saving faith provides an insistent motive to give thanks. This motive cannot be enforced; it is not just a moral virtue. There is no necessity for it; it is entirely voluntary. But it is not a subservient or complacent thankfulness. Sometimes we are urged to be thankful as a way of getting us to tolerate what should not be tolerated, and the demand for gratitude is rightly suspected by people who are hungry for justice. But it is the motive that makes all the difference. The person who works most closely with Jesus is not the person who is driven by uneasy conscience or even by compassionate anger. The motive which takes a person along with Jesus is the motive which says, 'We are full of thankfulness for the mercy and the promise of God; we express our thankfulness on behalf of all who do not have the words to do so themselves; and we will not be satisfied until everyone else has become so aware of the mercy and promise of God that they are thankful with us.'

And Luke tells us the story, to encourage us to discover faith and salvation in places where people may be suffering from some sort of double disability. Who is the tenth leper for you? Where are the Samaritans in our time and place?

For Working Groups

Ignition

There are several 'ways in' for such a story, and the leader can select whichever seems most appropriate.

What do you feel when you see a 'Keep Out' notice? What does it feel like when you disobey an instruction? What does it feel like when a group breaks up? What does it feel like when you are in a minority of one?

Exploration

This is a story about journeys and directions and boundaries. It is difficult to make out exactly what Luke was referring to in his account of the location – perhaps he was not familiar with the geography. But the general picture is clear enough. The movements within the story are important; they disclose the real point, and they can be worked out visually. You can use diagrams, on paper or on an overhead projector; or you can move models of people, or draughtsmen, across a board; or you can act out the movements on the floor of your meeting-place. You need to get the movements of the story – but not all the implications – clear in the minds of participants before getting into the work in teams.

Break into four teams:

1 Jesus
2 Lepers 1–9
3 Leper 10
4 Luke, our story-teller

Questions for Jesus:

What do you think about the ten and their different behaviours? What puzzles or surprises you? What are you learning? What (in this instance) do you mean when you use the words 'faith' and 'save'?

Questions for lepers 1–9:

Why do you behave as you do? What are your motives? What problems are caused to you by other participants in the story?

Questions for leper 10:

Why do you behave as you do? What actually happens to you? What obstacles or difficulties do you face? What do you think that Jesus is talking about when he uses the words 'faith' and 'save'?

Questions for Luke:

Why do you think that this story is going to be useful for your readers? Who do you think that your readers are going to

> *identify with? What do*
> *you understand (in*
> *this instance) by the*
> *words 'faith' and*
> *'save'?*

After a short time on these questions (between five and ten minutes), ask each of the first three teams to choose two members to go to visit another team.

- Members from the Jesus team visit lepers 1–9, and ask: *What do you think of me?*
- Members from the lepers 1–9 team visit leper 10, and ask: *What do you think of us? Why did we split up? Can we have anything to do with each other in future?*
- Members from leper 10 team visit Jesus, and ask: *What do you think of me? What do you mean when you tell me that my faith has saved me?*
- The Luke team splits up and goes to overhear the conversations between the other teams.

After another six or seven minutes, the visitors go back to their home teams. The members of the three teams tell each other what has been happening during the visiting process. The Luke team re-convenes, and members share with each other any points of interest. After two or three minutes, the group leader calls the whole group together, and asks the Luke team to explain what they think has been happening, and especially what they think is meant by the words 'faith' and 'save'.

Destination

Participants come back into the here-and-now, and return into their teams. The group leader will need to suggest questions that link the story to the specific here-and-now situation. These could include:

Who are the lepers for us? Who is being excluded, treated as an alien, stigmatized? How far do we contribute to this exclusion, and even depend upon it? How far, for instance, is the enormous difference between facilities for treating HIV/AIDS in Africa and in the West due to the continued impoverishment of Africa by the system of international debt?

How far is there, at our church, a 'keep out' sign (unspoken, unwritten, but perceived by those affected)? Who does not belong?

Where and how do we recognize faith and salvation? Where do we look?

How do you know whether a minority can be right?

How far do we feel ourselves to be 'saved'?

How far can we make our Eucharist a more inclusive and more heartfelt act of thanksgiving?

What implications, if any, are there for our life together as a church and for our church policies?

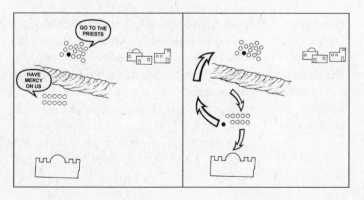

15

The Public Climb-Down

The Gospel Story

Luke 19:1–10

Narrator   Jesus went on into Jericho and was passing through. There was a chief tax collector there named Zacchaeus, who was rich. He was trying to see who Jesus was, but he was a little man and could not see Jesus because of the crowd. So he ran ahead of the crowd and climbed a sycamore tree to see Jesus, who was going to pass that way. When Jesus came to that place, he looked up.

Jesus   Hurry down, Zacchaeus, because I must stay in your house today.

Narrator   Zacchaeus hurried down and welcomed him with great joy. All the people who saw it started grumbling:

Grumbler   This man has gone as a guest to the home of a sinner!

Narrator
Zacchaeus   Zacchaeus stood up and said to the Lord: Listen, Sir! I will give half my belongings to the poor, and if I have cheated anyone, I will pay him back four times as much.

Jesus   Salvation has come to this house today, for this man, also, is a descendant of Abraham. The Son of Man came to seek and save the lost.

Making Connections

'Salvation' has always been an important word for theologians, from St Paul onwards. But the Saviour himself evidently used the word very little. In the Gospel records, the only occasion when he used the word about his own activities was in this story. So, if we want to see what Jesus himself thought about 'salvation', this must be the best place to look.

The main narrative in Luke's Gospel, after the prologue, starts at ch. 3, and that chapter begins with a list of the alien powers that were destroying the Jewish people's national identity. Control over money and foreign affairs had been taken over by Rome, represented by a military occupying power. Control over domestic affairs had passed into the hands of a few tribal chiefs, and control over the land had been taken by a small number of absentee landlords. Control over religious affairs was the responsibility of a toothless local priesthood, which was scornfully tolerated by Rome as a means of keeping the natives happy. The old system of God's law had broken down. It had insisted on God's authority over the basic sources of wealth, namely land and labour. The authority of God is the basis of the liberation laws in Leviticus 25, of Sabbath, release of debts, and Jubilee. These laws require that there be regular intervention, by conscious human initiative, to correct inequalities caused by the continual shifting in the distribution of wealth. Control of the land has to be regularly reviewed. Debt and enslavement have to be cancelled. Accumulation of money has to be limited. Commonsense wisdom tells us that accumulation causes wealth – indeed, that it *is* wealth. The standard objection to tax adjustments that would redistribute accumulated wealth is that they would be too expensive. Too expensive to *whom*? In the Leviticus laws, accumulation itself is too expensive – to the poor. It causes poverty, and has to be corrected by deliberate intervention in obedience to the design of the Creator. God is one who delivers his people from slavery. To be a slave is to be un-free, to be a being whose value is measured only in productive capacity and in surplus wealth generated in work performed for someone who controls. God is the Redeemer. He requires his people to behave as free people, both towards each other and towards the land.

All this is in the traditional culture for the Jewish people. They celebrated it and treasured it. But by the beginning of the Gospel story, the whole system had broken down, as we have seen. Into this gloomy situation, two new characters take the stage. First, John the Baptist, calling the whole community to take up its old allegiance to God's values; and then Jesus, with his Jubilee manifesto at Nazareth, announcing himself as the bringer of the Day of the Lord (Luke 4:18–19). He teaches, at the heart of his Kingdom-prayer, that only those who cancel their neighbours' debts can expect the divine forgiveness.

Jesus comes to a weary, depressed, disillusioned, divided nation, to people alienated from each other, from the land and from God. In the old days, the law of Moses had encouraged the people to hold the land in small units, so that the nation was a community of small-holders. But now, the Roman occupying power finds that it is easier to control a society based in a smaller number of large estates. This means that many people have lost their traditional land-rights. Some of these have moved up into the hills to become brigands or terrorists. Others just stay on as poor peasants; they are alienated from the wealth that their labour produces – but they at least may have some sense of belonging to a community, if only to a community of deprivation. But there are other members of the native community who seize the chance to collaborate with the colonists and exploit the situation to their individual advantage; they are also alienated. There are four features of this last group of people:

1 They are climbers; they are trying to detach themselves from the community of the poor and oppressed.
2 They get a niche in society by extracting wealth from the poorest and by sending it on to the owning or colonizing classes.
3 They are not employed to act in this way; in other words, they are not civil servants. They pay a fee to the owners and colonizers for the right to act in this way. Provided they send on sufficient money to the owners and colonizers, they can extract what they like from the peasants; they can make out their bills and invoices as they see fit.
4 So they are very isolated in their wealth. Their accumulation of wealth is directly related to the poverty of the peasants and tenants. This is what they depend on. Once they are in such a system, there is no escape for them.

It is no accident that Jesus tells so many stories about absentee landlords and oddly behaving employers. His hearers would recognize that this was all very close to their own experience. They would easily identify the kind of character that Jesus was talking about, in his story of the manager who gets into trouble with his plutocratic boss (Luke 16:1–9). This manager has secured a lucrative financial slot for himself, accumulating wealth for himself on the backs of the rent-paying peasants, who have to pay him a large percentage of the crops that they have produced by their labour. He uses his boss's assets to enrich himself by lending them out at high interest to poor people who are desperate for credit, and pocketing the profit. He is all right for as long as his luck holds out. But things start to go pear-shaped; he gets the 'or-else' from his plutocrat; and then he is alienated and isolated. He has trusted in an illusion; he has believed that the financial system can give him security. And it fails. But he has not been totally seduced by it. He retains a little commonsense. He realizes that he can't eat money, in the form of stocks and shares, or euros, or whatever. Where money-wealth lets him down, friendship-wealth may help him to survive. He can return to the community and solidarity of the poor by cancelling debts and forgoing the fees that he is due to collect from the peasants. In his own odd way, he can begin to act as an agent of the divine Jubilee, the Day of the Lord, in which indebtedness is to be abolished. So he calls in the invoices and adjusts the figures. He abandons the private profit that he has planned for himself. He ends up with no job, with nothing in his pocket; but the peasants will feel that, after all, he is on their side, so he will have enough goodwill to keep him in dinners and hospitality for the foreseeable future. He has called the bluff of the financial system. The economic structure of his life is no longer absorbing his destiny. He has exposed its false spirituality. He is no longer its victim. He is free.

There is hope even for this kind of person, Jesus tells us; he can be released and find a place within the community, if he himself acts as an agent of release. He has to stop trusting in a scheme of detaching himself from the general run of doomed humanity. But some sort of crisis is needed to steer him into making such a decision. It cannot be enforced by law. The presence of Jesus is the presence of the Kingdom of God's authority, the authority of the true owner and creator of the world and its wealth. Jesus brings the decisive crisis, the opportunity for repentance.

Commentators and preachers in the respectable Western world seem to find this parable obscure. But the situation can be recognized as true to life by anyone who has lived

within a colonized situation – such as was only too easy
to find in the British Isles a few generations ago. This
manager's activities are correctly described by the word
'squandered'. Jesus' hearers would have no difficulty in
recognizing the sort of person that he is describing. Such a
person would have his office just around the corner.

Which brings us to Zacchaeus. Here is not another
parable, but a real-life event. Here is another deeply alienated individual, a man with a Hebrew name in a Greek
form; he has sold himself as a financial agent to the colonial
overlords. He does not belong anywhere. He does not
belong to the Romans: for them, he is the convenient,
purchasable native. But he no longer belongs to his own
people; the rabbis taught that a Jew who collaborated with
the Gentiles by collecting taxes for them had made himself
a Gentile, no longer a member of the family of Abraham.

He has bought for himself the franchise for acting as a
tax-collector. The Roman colonizers decide how much he
must send on to them. Like colonizers everywhere, this is
what they are in business for; their project is to remove
wealth from the places of production and take it for their
own consumption. Provided that they get their rake-off,
they are satisfied. It is no business of theirs to decide how
much is actually to be taken from the peasants; the tax-
collector can decide that for himself. He will get as much as
he can, for his own pocket. Zacchaeus's career-pattern has
worked out well. He has risen successfully in this system; he
has farmed out much of his business to subordinate staff,
who pay him a substantial proportion of what they collect.
He has become an *architelones*, a superintendent tax-
collector, based in Jericho, a city which is both a centre of
trade and a pleasure-ground for the Roman occupying
force. In a word, he is rich.

In modern Britain, we have our friendly neighbourhood
Inspector of Taxes. Some may dislike what he stands for,
but we cannot blame him directly for the level of tax that is

required of us. Not so with Zacchaeus. His taxpayers have to pay what he decides, and it is a high rate – between 30 and 40 per cent of their income. From the point of view of the peasants, he, more than any other single factor, is the cause of their poverty. He has put himself irrevocably into the camp of the oppressors. He has climbed away from them, into his own isolated socio-economic nest. Like the manager in the parable, he has been seduced by an illusion, captured by a false spirituality. Zacchaeus has 'done well for himself' – as some would express it. Someone has to do the dirty jobs, and he is entitled to some reward. But he is himself a victim of the system. He is trapped in it. He believes that he can climb away from the general mess of the human race, in its poverty, misery and squalor. His great fear is that he will simply be absorbed into the majority, and have nothing distinctive or individual to show for himself. So he has chosen the way of isolation. He has been living with an illusion. He has been under the impression that he can be independent, that a financial device can give him protection from most human needs. But this sort of 'independence' is a lie. In fact, he is far more dependent on other people's labour than the majority of those who are poorer.

Jesus sees Zacchaeus, this horrible little man. For a considerable time, according to Luke, Jesus has been offering a gospel of Good News for the poor. He has taken a lot of trouble to project a face of God that will help the poor to feel that God is on their side, and not on the side of the religious police, the official guardians of social hygiene. Jesus is giving them the message that they are really free, that they are not fundamentally victims of religious or social or economic systems and prejudices. He has been willing to get into trouble with the authorities, in associating with people for whom the existing systems of power are giving no advantages. Now, for the sake of this one totally unpleasant character, he puts all this enterprise at risk.

There is little to be said in favour of Zacchaeus. The one thing to his credit is that he is curious. He is still sufficiently part of the general human race for him to take an interest in an unexpected novelty, the presence of Jesus, this strange man from the north. Moses was sufficiently curious to turn aside to see why a burning bush was not consumed (Exodus 3:3). Zacchaeus is curious enough to climb a tree, in order to get a view. Curiosity can be the beginning of a miracle, a deliverance.

Modern readers will be understandably curious about the tree. For us in Britain, 'sycamore' means a kind of large maple tree, common enough, but formidable for a skilled woodsman to climb, let alone a short, respectably dressed businessman taking time off from his office. For some perverse reason, we have lifted this word 'sycamore' from its original Mediterranean meaning and applied it to our northern European tree. Luke gives us the word 'syco-more', which means literally a 'fig-mulberry'. It is mentioned occasionally in the Old Testament. It was a common type of fig tree, often to be found on the wayside in that part of the world, with a short stocky trunk and low spreading branches – an ideal tree for even little Zacchaeus to climb.

And there must be some curiosity in the mind of Jesus. He is on a very definite journey; he is almost at the end of his pilgrimage to the Holy City. He is becoming aware of the final crisis that he must present to the authorities there, and is just passing through a strange and unappealing town. Then he sees this little man up a tree. And he is willing to be diverted.

Jesus speaks directly to Zacchaeus. Occasionally, our Gospel-writers give us the actual words of Jesus, when there is an especially significant word in Aramaic. We hear him saying *'Talitha koum'* – 'Girl, get up'; *'Ephphatha'* – 'Be opened'. Jesus is working in an environment where the Greek language also was frequently used, especially in commercial contexts. Jesus would surely have some competence in Greek. Peasants and artisans have often got a wider range of languages than people with more sophisticated schooling. (In South Africa, I remember well how a Zulu petrol-pump attendant would be able to talk in Zulu, Sotho, English and Afrikaans, whereas an expensively educated white person might have no real competence in any language other than English. A similar point is made, using the example of nineteenth-century Irish peasants, by Oscar Wilde.[1]) So I reckon that it is quite possible that Jesus would find it appropriate to speak to Zacchaeus in Greek, and that we are hearing his actual words – '*Speusas katabethi*'.

These words of command of Jesus are very significant; this is why the Gospel-writers take such care in giving them. Get up; take up your bed; be opened; peace, be still. To Zacchaeus, the significant command is 'Come down quickly. Come down. Leave your nest up there. Come and join us on the floor. Come and join me; make your journey downwards, join the rest of the human race, abandon your project of creating a niche of security for yourself measured by the distance between yourself and the rest of us. Come down. I am taking your side. I am coming to eat with you. Your salvation is not to be in separation from the poor but in community with the poor. Salvation is not an escape-route from the common lot of human beings, but a way of belonging to them more deeply.'

From his place among the poor, at the foot of the tree, Jesus calls Zacchaeus. Zacchaeus comes down and joins him. The poor are offended and lose confidence in Jesus. It is not the Scribes and Pharisees who complain; it's the general public. The 'deserving poor' may be the sharpest critics of the 'undeserving'. When Zacchaeus joins Jesus, the general public move away. If you draw the line at Zacchaeus, you find that you have drawn the line at Jesus.

Jesus is not embarrassed to expose his own neediness – he

wants a dinner. And Zacchaeus is freed to respond. In calling him to 'Come down', Jesus is not asking him to surrender his unique distinctiveness as a person. He is offering the salvation of God.

Zacchaeus responds because Jesus puts himself at risk and treats him as a real person, and so accepts his hospitality. The effect is that he engages in voluntary justice. He hands over half of his capital to the poor. From the other half, he undertakes to pay fourfold reimbursement for any cheating or fraud. This is the maximum fine that can be imposed by the courts on a convicted thief, in Roman and Jewish law. His giving to the poor is not compassion; it is justice. He is restoring to the poor what is rightly theirs. He is treating his financial activities as if they were criminal robberies. At the same time, he is doing this as a free moral agent. In Martin Luther King's fine phrase, he 'rises to the majestic heights of the unenforceable'. He is not under legal compulsion. This is specifically what Jesus describes as 'salvation'. Jesus does not merely tell Zacchaeus that he is saved. He gives an experience that conveys the meaning of salvation. He restores Zacchaeus to a place among the inheritors. In spite of his past behaviour, Zacchaeus has not, in fact, been cut off from the people of God. His security is guaranteed, not by his moral standing but by the reckless generosity of Jesus, not by his success in separating himself from the poverty and deprivation of the general mass of humanity but by his being willing to be poor again among the poor. It is his house, which has suddenly lost most of its wealth, and not the homes of the poor who have suddenly heard the promise of unexpected refunds, which is stated to be the place of salvation.

Zacchaeus has been a notorious and conspicuous member of that category known as 'sinners'. Sin is a debt, owed to God, and Zacchaeus is very deep in such debt. There was a recognized procedure for the rehabilitation of such people, even such evident sinners as Zacchaeus. It was expensive and lengthy, and was operated by the religious establishment, according to the laws. But Jesus is bringing the Kingdom, the day of God's gracious release. He bypasses the whole religious process, and makes it unnecessary. Zacchaeus's self-imposed fines will leave him even poorer than the Temple's penalties would; but they will go direct to the poor peasants, not into the well-supplied coffers of the priesthood. On the last leg of his journey to Jerusalem, Jesus will scarcely find that this sort of behaviour will endear him to the central guardians of religious morality in the capital city.

Often, where Jesus speaks of someone being 'saved', this is when something happens which we would call a miracle, an event of healing that goes beyond our human compe-tence. But the Gospel-writers do not have a distinct category of 'miracle-stories'. What happens to Zacchaeus is just as much an event of salvation as the healing of a paralytic, just as miraculous as the recovery of sight to the blind. For such a person to be thus restored to wholeness was, according to the rabbis, as improbable as raising the dead.

In the Gospel of Mark, a very rich man approaches Jesus, seeking eternal life (in telling the story, Mark switches from 'entering eternal life' to 'entering the Kingdom of God' to 'being saved', with very much the same meaning). Unlike Zacchaeus, he does not appear to be a man who has devoted a lot of practical energy to getting rich; he simply *is* rich. He can come at life with the effortless superiority of one who does not have to worry about money; he can take his economic dominance for granted, and so can look at the world with the eye of a man who is used to being obeyed. He has the natural attractiveness of the privileged young who can afford to be idealistic. Because he has no need to concern himself with the processes of production of wealth, he has the spare energy to devote to religious achievement. He can claim, no doubt truthfully, that he has been keep-ing all the rules which ordinary religious people keep –

something that Zacchaeus could certainly not claim. But he is looking for something more – a more exclusive religion, on a higher mystical plane, or at a more extreme level of purity (among religious Jews in those days, people with a lot of money were often very keen on the detailed rules of purity). He is looking for a spiritual achievement to count to his credit, to match his economic accumulation. But he has not learned of Jesus' teaching, that mammon is to be seen as a rival divinity to the true God (Matthew 6:24). We are told that Jesus feels *love* for this man; evidently this is a unique moment – nowhere else in the first three Gospels do we hear that Jesus loves someone. And then Jesus goes on immediately to tell him that his solution has to be not in the area of spiritual exercises but in the mundane realm of his economic status. He has to hand over all his wealth to the poor, become some kind of drop-out, and join the odd bunch of characters called Disciples. What an overwhelming disappointment, not only to the man but doubtless also to the Disciples – they could do with having a wealthy patron. So they ask whether there is actually anyone for whom salvation is attainable. If it's virtually impossible for the rich, what chance is there for 'ordinary' folk like themselves (Mark 10:26)? The story of Zacchaeus provides an answer. In spite of his wealth, he is loveable. With God, salvation is possible, even for the rich.

For Working Groups

Ignition

Either

If you are in a group where you can move around a little, put the tallest people to stand in the front row and the shortest behind, and let the leader draw something and talk about it to the front row. What do the short people feel like?

What do the short people feel like in a crowd?

Or
Why have you ever climbed trees?

Exploration

The leader can briefly describe the role and motives of a chief tax-collector, and point out how this story comes almost at the end of Jesus' journey to Jerusalem. It might be helpful for a summary of the movements in the Zacchaeus story to be expressed by means of a diagram drawn on the overhead projector or flipchart.

Break into four teams:

1 Jesus
2 Zacchaeus
3 The general public and the Disciples
4 Luke, our story-teller

Questions for Jesus:

What are you doing here, in Jericho? Where have you come from? Where are you going? What problems do you face as you decide what to do about Zacchaeus? What do you mean when you speak of 'salvation'?

Questions for
Zacchaeus:

What is your opinion of Jesus at the beginning of the story? What do you really want? What change happens to you in the course of the story? What are you actually doing when you make your announcement about money at the end of the story? Why do you make this decision? What is going to be the effect on you?

Questions for the
general public and
the Disciples:

What is your opinion of Jesus at the beginning of the story? What is your opinion of Jesus at the end of the story? What do you think about the various stages of the story?

Questions for Luke:

Why do you tell this story? What use do you think it is going to be for the Church for which you are writing? What do you think is meant by the word 'salvation' at the end of the story? What sort of people are likely to correspond with the character of Zacchaeus in the Church for which you are writing?

After a few minutes of getting into the roles of the characters, let each team choose one or two representatives to visit another team. The opening questions for all visitors are: *What do you think of us? What problems do we cause you?*

· Members from the Jesus team visit the general public and Disciples.
· Members from the general public and Disciples team visit Zacchaeus.
· Members from the Zacchaeus team visit Jesus.
· The Luke team splits up and goes to overhear the conversations between the other teams.

After a few minutes, the teams re-convene and share their feelings. When the whole group re-assembles, let the Luke team comment on the attitude of the general public and Disciples, and express their understanding of the meaning of the word 'salvation'.

Either at this stage, or at the end of the whole meeting, if you have space, re-enact the story simply. Start with Jesus (the Jesus team) standing surrounded by the general public and Disciples team at one end of the room, and the Zacchaeus team as far away as possible at the other end.

Jesus calls to Zacchaeus, 'Come down. Come here. Quick!'

Zacchaeus moves down the room to stand alongside Jesus.

The onus then is on the general public and Disciples; will they stay with Jesus and Zacchaeus? Or will they be so unhappy about being with Zacchaeus that they move away not only from Zacchaeus but also from Jesus? Where can they move to? Only to the place vacated by Zacchaeus!

Destination

Who might Zacchaeus be for us, in our day and in our place? Are we Zacchaeus? How should the Church, the Body of Christ, respond to such a person?

How do we not only tell people that they are saved but also give them an experience that tells them that they are saved?

'The question to be asked is not what we should give to the poor but how can we stop taking from the poor. The poor are not our problem; we are their problem.'[2] How does this affect the way we think about such matters as the remission of the debts of the poorest nations, and the support of trading schemes which will enable poor communities to have a fair access to the markets of the richer world?

Are we rich? What hope is there for us? For Jesus, poverty is not a problem; but affluence is.

We are used to ecumenical and ecclesiastical questions such as: How can those who disagree with the ordination of women to the priesthood share communion with those who accept the ordination of women to the priesthood? How can those who accept the authority of the Pope share communion with those who do not accept the authority of the Pope? But these questions are trivial, compared with the question: How can those who are poor share communion with those who make them poor?

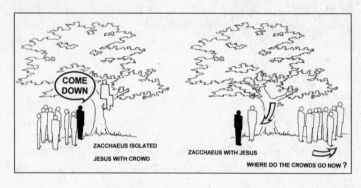

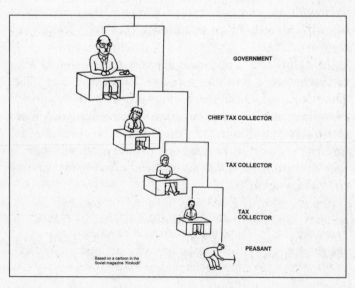

16

The Blind who Sees

The Gospel Story

Mark 10:46–52

Narrator	They came to Jericho. As Jesus was leaving Jericho, with his disciples and a large crowd, the son of Timaeus, Bartimaeus, a blind beggar, sat by the wayside. When he heard that it was Jesus of Nazareth, he began to shout and say:
Bartimaeus	Son of David, Jesus, have mercy on me!
Narrator	Many scolded him and warned him to be silent. But he shouted much more:
Bartimaeus	Son of David, have mercy on me.
Narrator	And Jesus stopped and said:
Jesus	Call him.
Narrator	And they called the blind man, saying to him:
Crowd	Take heart, get up, he is calling you.
Narrator	He threw away his cloak, jumped up, and went to Jesus. Jesus responded to him saying:
Jesus	What do you want me to do for you?
Narrator	The blind man said to him:
Bartimaeus	Rabbuni, that I may see again.
Narrator	And Jesus said to him:

Jesus   Go, your faith has saved you.
Narrator   And immediately he did see again, and
                  followed him in the way.

Making Connections

Bartimaeus suffers from a double disability. He has lost his sight. And he has lost his ability to earn a living. His request is correctly translated as 'that I may see *again*'. He once was sighted; he can remember what it was like to be able to see, so he has some visual memory. But, like many who become blind, he has also become unemployed. He is an outsider to the community of holiness; he could not qualify to be a priest. And he is an outsider to the community of work and production. He has to live on other people's surplus wealth. In his own abilities, he is useless.

He has set up his begging-pitch on the edge of Jericho, hoping to catch the passing trade. This was a prudent choice. Jericho was a lively place, a resort for off-duty Roman soldiers. As the so-called parable of the Good Samaritan shows, the 15-mile road downhill from Jerusalem was one that was taken by travellers who were worth ambushing by brigands. And it was the place where the chief tax-collector, Zacchaeus, had his office.

Jesus is on the last leg of his journey to Jerusalem – a time of increasing anxiety and tension. The Disciples are with him, but they are absorbed into a large body of other people. The word translated 'crowd' means not so much the citizens of the place but the poor peasants, the people of the land, who had little security under the Roman occupation. The blind man is sitting on the ground by the roadside. He has a cloak. It could be a cast-off from a Roman soldier, or something picked up cheap at the Army Surplus Stores. A beggar has to make do with what no one else wants. In the heat of the day, he does not need the cloak in order to keep warm; he spreads it out in front of him to catch the odd coin that someone might throw. It corresponds to the modern beggar's cap or the busker's guitar-case. He can hear that something significant is going on. He is aware that a greater number of people than usual is milling around; he can hear their feet and their voices, but he cannot detect what is actually happening. Eventually he discovers that the commotion is being caused by the presence of Jesus of Nazareth. Jesus has not been in Jericho before; Bartimaeus can have heard of him only through the stories passed around, which he has overheard. But he immediately starts to call on Jesus as Messiah. No one else has done so in public in that area. He cannot see his way into pushing through the crowd and locating Jesus. His blindness immobilizes. So he shouts. The general public, the crowd, with the disciples, are thoroughly discouraging. But his voice is the one useful faculty at his disposal, and he makes good use of it.[1]

Jesus hears a voice addressing him as Son of David, the title meaning 'Messiah'. He has previously talked about this role with the Disciples, but very confidentially; and this is not the voice of one of the Disciples. It is not, as in the case of the Syro-Phoenician woman, the voice of a Greek from the north. The only other voice that, up to now, has addressed him as Messiah has been the voice of demons; and this is certainly not the voice of a demon. It is a cry for help.

Jesus stops still, so that he can easily be located. He overrules the disciples and the crowd who have been trying to silence Bartimaeus, and tells them to call him. They obey. They tell him, 'Cheer up' – don't be discouraged, get up, he's calling you. They are messengers of salvation to him. The calling of Jesus draws Bartimaeus out of his immediate pre-occupations, his hopes for getting a few coins to pay for a supper. He throws away his cloak; he abandons his only means of getting money; he gives up his role and occupation as beggar. He gets onto his feet; as a blind person, his feet are a vital method of feeling where he is. He moves towards the source of the voice that has said 'Call him'. The crowd makes way for him.

Jesus requires him to put himself into words. 'What do you want from me?' This kind of question can be heard in many ways, depending mainly on the tone of voice in which it is spoken. It can be a general enquiry. It can be an accusation. It can be sympathetic. It can be irritated or impatient. Trainee actors practise saying such a phrase with many different inflections. We can speculate about this if we are so minded. Bartimaeus, as a blind person, is skilled at detecting such nuances, and he understands Jesus' question as a straight enquiry. What does he want? The normal answer to be expected from a blind beggar would be, 'Cash'. If the question is being put by a religious leader, the answer might be, 'Can you get me a place in a hostel?' If the question is being put by the police, the answer might be, 'Can you organize transport for me to get back to my sister's?' But Bartimaeus is speaking to the Messiah, the one who is bringing in the Day of the Lord and the Kingdom of God. The request to the Messiah can only be, 'I want my sight back.' Jesus replies, 'Go' – you are free to move on your own feet and without a guide. 'Your faith has saved you.' You have not seen me; and 'faith is the conviction of things not seen' and 'blessed are those who have not seen and yet have believed'. The blind man actually has an advantage; he is not rubbish, useless, 'dis-abled'. He is in the image of God, who 'sees in secret'. He is the true model of faith (Hebrews 11:1; John 20:29; Matthew 6:4, 6). Immediately, Bartimaeus sees again; he follows Jesus, in the way.

Bartimaeus has been excluded from society by a double disability: he has been blind, and he has been a beggar. He is now restored to a place within the 'normal' fabric of humanity, and this includes his place within the market. He has a new access to 'normal' work and exchange. This is one of the signs of the Kingdom; people and communities are delivered from a beggar-role. This is reflected in the achievements of the Fair Trade movement, since its tiny beginnings in a greengrocer's shop in 1979. It is not just another 'cause' for giving to the poor; it is a programme for enabling the rich world to stop taking from the poor, by enabling the poor to have access to world markets. Goods are on sale on supermarket shelves, which would not have been there only a couple of years ago. The movement is still tiny, as was the Christian movement in its first few months. But it is a sign of an alternative approach to trading.

In the story that immediately precedes the story of Bartimaeus in Mark's Gospel, we hear Jesus asking almost exactly the same question, 'What do you want me to do for you?' On this occasion, he is replying to two of his closest friends who want him to organize top jobs for them in Jesus' future government. He has to respond to them with disappointment. They are his disciples; right at the beginning, he called them; they have had all the privileges of association with Jesus, and have had a unique opportunity to understand who he is and how he operates. They have also had normal eyesight with which to observe him. But, in comparison with Bartimaeus, they are blind. When Bartimaeus recognizes Jesus, all they can do is to get in the way, obstructing, discouraging. This is nothing new. Mark is painfully honest in recording the general stupidity, obstructiveness and incomprehension of the disciples. Evidently, this was a necessary message for the Churches for which Mark wrote; they also must have had to put up with stupid, discouraging and uncomprehending leadership. And doubtless there is something in this same message for us in our day. At the same time, there have been, and still are, the Bartimaeuses, the blind who see better than the sighted – and the deaf who listen better than the hearing, the lame who move more freely than the able-bodied, and the people with learning difficulties who understand better than the intelligent.

Bartimaeus becomes a disciple. He follows Jesus, as those unreliable earlier Disciples did, 'in the way'. By the time that the Gospel was written, 'the Way' was one of the most common terms for referring to the Christian movement, the community of discipleship. This is salvation; this is the effect of faith. As in other places in the Gospel text, some English versions translate the word for 'save' as 'make well' or 'heal'; but this is to weaken Mark's language. Bartimaeus's sight is restored; but salvation is more than a return to a previous state of well-being; it is not just a restoration onto the screen from the recycle-bin. It is a sharing in the new thing, the Kingdom of justice and of access to the gifts of the Creator.

This is the last event in the story of Jesus, before he arrives at the entry-point for Jerusalem.

For Working Groups

Ignition

Put the question to the members: Why are you here? How do you pronounce this question? Try out different ways of saying it. How does it sound?

Suppose that it is, in fact, asked in a friendly and sympathetic manner. What is your answer? Why, in fact, are you here? What do you come to this meeting for? What do you expect?

Exploration

Read the story, and note one or two main points, especially the 'double disability' of being blind and being dependent on begging. Also note the contrast between

the blind man's insight and the sighted Disciples' blindness in the previous story in Mark 10.

Break into four teams:

1 Bartimaeus
2 Jesus
3 The Disciples/general public/crowd
4 Mark, our story-teller

Questions for Bartimaeus:	*What sort of person are you? What are your main interests and motives – both in general and in the opening of this story? What is happening to you? What are the options open to you in the course of the story? What makes you choose to act as you do?*
Questions for Jesus:	*How does Bartimaeus fit into your plans at this point? How do you feel about the claim which he makes? Why do you respond as you do? What is the purpose of your question? What do you mean by your last statement? What are you recognizing when you speak of 'faith', and what do you mean by 'save'?*

Questions for the Disciples/
general public/crowd: *Why are you there? What*
are your main interests?
What makes you respond
to Bartimaeus as you do?
What is your estimate of
Jesus? Does it change in
the course of the story?

Questions for Mark: *What, for you, is the*
main point of this story –
especially as your last
story before Jesus' entry
into Jerusalem? What do
you understand by the
words 'faith' and 'save'
in the last statement of
Jesus? Why do you think
this story is going to be
useful for the Church for
which you are writing?

After sufficient time for these questions, the teams
choose representatives for visiting each other. The
opening question for all visitors is: *In what way do I/we*
present a demand or problem to you?

· Members from the Jesus team visit the Disciples/
general public/crowd.
· Members from the Disciples/general public/crowd
team visit Bartimaeus.
· Members from the Bartimaeus team visit Jesus.
· The Mark team splits up and goes to overhear the
conversations between the other teams.

The teams re-assemble. Mark leads the discussion,
based on the Mark team's last two questions.

Destination

Do you see this sort of pattern happening in your church, that is, the relationship between the 'blind' and the 'sighted', the people with few advantages and the people with many?

How far is your church accessible to blind and partially sighted people? How good is the visibility? How easy is the place to feel one's way around, to find such things as the entrances, the cloakrooms, steps, etc.? Have you consulted a blind person, or an advisor, about this sort of matter?

Does your church organization put its newsletter onto cassette?

How far are you involved with programmes to deliver people and communities from the 'beggar-role', by Fair Trade, ethical investment programmes, political pressure-groups, etc.?

Another word with the Evangelist

A further extract from the interview between Dudley and the Evangelist Mark.

Dudley	I have another problem, Sir. You give us all these individual stories, but it all looks so unsystematic. Wouldn't you agree that what people need is a proper and coherent statement of what salvation really means?
Mark	Well, there were people in my time who felt that way. They wanted better definitions. They reckoned that if we could get more definitions, more

qualifications for membership, we would be more competitive with the rest of the religious market.

Dudley I think that this is just the sort of thing we are looking for – the first real systematic theology. If you can share this information with me, I can work it up into a thesis of incomparable significance, and I will be happy to put a word in for you in the Acknowledgements.

Mark Well, let me tell you how they got on. I mentioned that I was keen to meet that Simon, so I trailed off on the long road to Cyrene. When I got there, I found that there were two young comrades, brothers they were, called Rufus and Alexander, Simon's sons. They were dead keen to attend some big get-together that the management was arranging, in Antioch or some such place, to go into this whole issue of salvation that you're so keen on. They reckoned that if they could get themselves selected to go to this affair as delegates, when they got back they might have a good chance of promotion to be some sort of Rural Dean of the Presbyters. So they were putting themselves forward for this slice of action, at this big get-together in Cyrene. And then, in the middle of the meeting, there came a voice, rather shrill it was, from the edge of the room, and it was calling out loud,

'Hi, everyone, I'm Marcella. I hope I've come to the right place. Is it right that Brother John Mark from Jerusalem is here?'

So, of course, I said at once, 'Sure, Sister Marcella; I'm here.'

'Mark,' she said, 'I've heard that you've got a collection of stories about the Master.'

'Right enough,' I answered.

'Well then,' she said, 'tell them the one about James and John. See what those up-front characters make of that.'

Now then, I thought quickly, she can't mean the one about how Jesus called James and John at the beginning, because Peter and Andrew were in that one, just as much. All I could think of was the one about when James and John tried to bend Jesus' ear to make them top dog.

Dudley   We have another version of this story, which tells us that it was their mother that was really to blame.

Mark   I don't go for that. I don't think Jesus would blame the mother. He went straight for those two cleverlegs and gave them a right earful. But I didn't see what this had to do with faith and salvation, which was what the meeting was supposed to be about, so I went straight on to tell them about that blind beggar, Bartimaeus. I reckon he saw what James and John and co. didn't see.

Dudley	So what happened next?
Mark	Well, no one spoke for a minute or two. Then Rufus said, rather slowly, 'So that's what happened to James and John, is it? Well now . . .'
	And Alexander, a bit sharply, I thought, called out, 'Who asked for that story to be told?'
	And Marcella immediately chirped up from the edge of the room, 'Is that Alexander? I'm Marcella, and I asked for the story to be told, and I'm not apologizing, either. If the cap fits . . .'
	And Alexander came back at her, 'I'm not asking you to apologize, but I think that if we're going to send anyone to this conference it should be you.'
	And Marcella answered, 'I couldn't possibly do that. I'm only a slave-girl, and my master wouldn't give me that much time off. It's bad enough trying to get to a meeting like this. And any road, I couldn't go, because I'm blind.'
Dudley	Ah, that's why she was so keen to get people's names spelled out.
Mark	Good for you, young man, to have spotted that.
Dudley	One of my teachers in Birmingham was blind, and he alerted us to that sort of thing.[2]
Mark	He did right. The Master was very keen to give proper place to folks that the topside gentry call 'disabled'. Alexander, fair play to him, had picked

that up all right. He told Marcella
straightaway, 'As far as I'm concerned,
that's all the more reason why you
should be there. From what we've
heard today, there are things that
people like you know about faith,
which the rest of us just miss out on.'

Dudley   So, did she go? Did the great consultation about salvation take place?

Mark   Sorry to disappoint you, my friend, but
I don't think it did come off, not till
well after my time, anyway. No. We
just kept on looking at the times when
Jesus talked about faith and salvation
and suchlike, and all the time it was
about exceptions. All the people concerned were exceptions to this or that.
They never seemed to have any kind of
qualification. So there's your systematic for you. How can you organize an
office on the basis of exceptions, I ask
you – especially when the gaffer is an
exception to all the qualifications
himself?

Perhaps, later on, they might get
round to the sort of thing you're on
about. But all we could do at that
stage was just to go on collecting stories. There's no single story is going to
give you a magic formula for your
qualifications; but, we reckoned, if we
put them together we'll get a load of
different pictures, and perhaps it will
all add up.

17

Talent-Spotting

This is a design for a practical conference, for between 18 and 40 people, lasting for between one-and-a-quarter hours and two hours. The total membership meets together in one room at the start. But then immediately the total membership is divided into two groups, of exactly equal numbers. For the first 40–45 minutes, these meet separately, in different rooms if possible. Group A, but not Group B, will probably need to have the use of an overhead projector.

Group A meets with a leader to consider the last parable that Jesus tells, the parable of the gold coins, according to Luke's scheme of the Gospel (dramatized text follows below). Each member is given two copies of the parable. The group leader explains that the reason for the second copy will emerge later.

The Gospel Story

Luke 19:12–26

Narrator	Jesus told them a parable. He was now almost at Jerusalem, and they supposed that the Kingdom of God was just about to appear. So he said:
Jesus	There was once a man of high rank who was going to a country far away to be

made king, after which he planned to come back home. Before he left, he called his ten servants and gave them each a gold coin and told them:

King   See what you can earn with this while I am gone.

Jesus   The man was made king and came back. At once he ordered his servants to appear before him, in order to find out how much they had earned. The first one came and said:

Servant 1   Sir, I have earned ten gold coins with the one you gave me.

King   Well done; you are a good servant! Since you were faithful in small matters, I will put you in charge of ten cities.

Jesus   The second servant came and said:

Servant 2   Sir, I have earned five gold coins with the one you gave me.

King   You will be in charge of five cities.

Jesus   Another servant came and said:

Servant 3   Sir, here is your gold coin; I kept it hidden in a handkerchief. I was afraid of you, because you are a hard man. You take what is not yours and reap what you did not sow.

King   You bad servant! I will use your own words to condemn you! You know that I am a hard man, taking what is not mine and reaping what I have not sown. Well, then, why didn't you put my money in the bank? Then I would have received it back with interest when I returned.

Jesus   Then he said to those who were standing there:

King   Take the gold coin away from him and

	give it to the servant who has ten coins.
Jesus	But they said to him:
Person	Sir, he already has ten coins!
Jesus	The king replied:
King	I tell you, that to every person who has something, even more will be given; but the person who has nothing, even the little that he has will be taken away from him.

Making Connections

According to Luke's story, Jesus and the disciples are very close to the end of their journey to Jerusalem. Their pilgrimage is almost over. The disciples expect to see the results of their hardships and their commitment. For them, the Kingdom is just around the corner, and salvation and deliverance are going to be their reward. But they have misunderstood Christ's timing. There will be new commitments, new opportunities and new risks.

So Jesus gives them a final parable. Like most of the parables, it is not a simple story-with-a-moral. It does not yield one obvious lesson. It is an awkward story, which has some unattractive implications if it is pressed with too much logic. (In the version printed here, we have tried to disentangle a confusion that apparently has got into Luke's text; in the full version printed in Bibles, there is another parable being told at the same time, about a king's punitive reprisals against some stirrers of civic disorder.) The parable is a story and a situation that Jesus puts before the Disciples (and therefore before us), in effect asking, 'Who are you in this story? How do you fit in? What does it say about you?'

For Working Groups

Exploration

Group A starts by reading the text.

Then break into three teams:

1 King
2 Servants 1 and 2
3 Servant 3

Questions for each team:

> *What sort of person are we? What are our main motives? Why do we behave as we do? What do we think about the other characters in the story?*

After a few minutes to get into the characters, each team selects one or two members to visit another team. The opening questions for all visitors are: *What do you think of me? Am I right or wrong? What is there in the future for us?*

· Members from the servants 1 and 2 team visit the King.
· Members from the servant 3 team visit servants 1 and 2.
· Members from the King team visit servant 3.

When this has gone on long enough, the visitors return to their teams, and briefly share their experiences. The three teams then take on new characters:

1 Jesus
2 The Disciples
3 Luke, our story-teller

Questions for Jesus:	*Why do I tell this story? What am I trying to put across?*
Questions for the Disciples:	*What is Jesus up to? What is the parable saying to us?*
Questions for Luke:	*Why do I think that this parable is worth passing on to my readers? What are they going to make of it – especially at this point in my total story?*

The three teams work on these questions for a few minutes, and then come together as one group.

For the final phase, the group leader draws the whole discussion together, with the members playing Luke giving answers to his questions. The following points ought to be drawn out:

Even if you feel fairly satisfied with your church – if you feel that it has 'arrived', don't assume that your present state of things is fixed and final and permanent – there will be new adventures to be undertaken, and therefore new risks to be ventured.

Your 'gifts' are all *loans*; what you possess, as individuals and as a church, is not yours to possess and to use for your own advantage. You are accountable to your Creator for these gifts. Don't just be content with making platitudes about 'using your God-given talents'. On whose account are you using them, as individuals and as a church? What have you been 'burying'?

There should always be a proper risk of loss; you are not primarily in business to *preserve* anything. Look, for instance, at your church budget: how much is for preservation and how much for growth and transformation? (The one thing wasted, in the Gospels, is the hundredweight-and-a-half of spices with which faithful people tried to preserve the corpse of Jesus.)

What, in practice, are our 'gifts' as a church community? Make a list.

As a church, how well are we using the 'gifts' with which we are entrusted?

Group B meets separately. It starts by reading through Paul's account of the gifts of the Spirit in 1 Corinthians 12. Then each member is given a series of 24 questions, and a grid on which to write in the answers. This should be done by members individually. There is no need for absolute silence, but each member should take responsibility for the scores and totals that he/she records. Each member is given two copies of the questionnaire and the grid. At this stage, they use just one copy of each; they will be told later what to do with the other one.

Acknowledging Some of your Gifts

How to Complete the Questionnaire

Take each statement in turn and ask yourself, 'Is this statement true in my life and experience?' Then indicate your score according to the following scale, writing the appropriate number in the corresponding square of the table (see p. 204):

Greatly..........	3	Little............	1
Some.............	2	Not at all......	0

After you have completed the test by rating yourself for each of the 24 statements, add the scores in each horizontal row. Record the sum in the 'Total' column. Your total score for each row indicates your level of interest in that particular 'gift'. The final column, 'Significance', is not to be used at this point. It is to be filled in later, after discussion about the meaning of the scoring.

When everyone has finished recording their scores, the group leader will conduct a discussion on the significance of the scores, and members will try to work out what gift each row represents.

1 I have a deep concern to encourage people towards spiritual growth.
2 I enjoy studying the Christian faith and sharing it with others.
3 I am always ready to overlook my own interests so that the needs of others may be met.
4 I am able to manage my financial affairs well, so that I can give generously for God's concerns.
5 I find it easy to delegate responsibility.
6 I enjoy visiting those in hospital and the housebound.

7 I find my contribution helps people towards a further searching for truth.

8 I am concerned that truth should be presented in a clear and intelligible way.

9 I can make people feel at ease.

10 I am concerned that financial resources be available for all sections of the Church.

11 I am able to supervise effectively the activities of others.

12 I have a great concern for those in trouble.

13 I stand up for the truth whenever there is an opportunity.

14 I am diligent in my study of the Bible and in any necessary research for it.

15 I am a good listener.

16 I am careful with money and pray for its proper distribution according to God's purposes.

17 I am glad to supply people with information that will help them to work effectively.

18 I work well with those who are ignored by the majority.

19 I am able to share the word of God with sincerity and conviction.

20 I am interested in finding new and useful ways in presenting biblical and Christian truth.

21 I am aware of my prejudices and relate sympathetically to people who are different from me.

22 I am willing to have my time claimed.

23 I am sensitive to the need for a smoothly run administration.

24 I can relate to others emotionally, and help when help is needed.

				Total	Significance
A	1	7	13	19		
B	2	8	14	20		
C	3	9	15	21		
D	4	10	16	22		
E	5	11	17	23		
F	6	12	18	24		

Some members will be surprised at their scores and at the implications of them. They will realize that they have gifts that previously they had not identified.

Eventually, there should be agreement on the 'Significance'. In the light of this discussion, members may wish to go through the exercise a second time, and see if they score themselves differently. At the end, members will be able to see more positively how their gifts can be used in the continuing work of salvation.

(The 'Significance' of the scores, as we understand it, is not included at this point. We urge you, the reader, to do this exercise, and think out for yourself what the scores mean for you. We include our interpretation of the scores in the Notes at the end of this book, but don't cheat!)[1]

The two programmes, for Group A and Group B working separately and simultaneously, should take about 40 or 50 minutes. Then it would be sensible to have a coffee-break. However, the leaders of each group should firmly instruct their members not to discuss with the other group what they have been doing.

When everyone re-convenes after the break, the total membership meets again in one room and the group leader introduces the following procedure. Each member of Group A is to find a partner from Group B; they get together with each other in pairs. The member from Group B gives his/her spare copy of the questionnaire and the grid to the member from Group A, and takes the member from Group A through the procedure, in the same way as the leader of Group B has done. In pairs, this will take probably 20–25 minutes. Then, in the same pairs, the member from Group A will give the member from Group B a copy of the parable, and will give an account of the process that Group A followed.

By the end of this procedure, every member will have been through the questionnaire about individual 'gifts', and will have some idea of the way the parable can be used as an examination of the motives and priorities of the corporate fellowship of the Church. Moreover, each member will have had the experience of being a communicator of what they have just previously learned. At one time, we as group leaders used to do our own bit twice, but then we realized that it would be more profitable if we immediately treated the members as teachers. Therefore the group leaders are not active for a period of about 40 minutes, but they need to keep a look out for any difficulties, and to ensure, for example, that there is a proper change-over so that the Group B members hear what happened in Group A.

Destination

If this process can lead into a specific discussion about
the task of the local church and its individual members,
the following questions could lead to practical policy-
making.

1. What is the 'talent' or 'gift' that we, as the
church community, have been entrusted with? Are we
preserving it? Are we using it? Are we risking it so that
it can grow?

2. We have people with a lot of different skills, abilities and experiences. How far do we know what
resources of this kind we have? Could we be making
better use of them by a little more conscious planning?
How carefully, for instance, are the members of our
church council and its committees chosen?

How well does our church use its ministers? Do they
feel that they are able to give all that they should be
giving? Is the church helping them to be efficient and to
improve their skills?

How far are our members able to use and share their
experience – for instance, their experience of conflict, of
struggle with unbelief, of being on the wrong side of the
prevailing systems, of discovering the meaning of faith
in the context of work and employment, of bereave-
ment, of sickness, of parenthood, of other cultures and
languages, etc.?

3. We all have time. In particular, our time together
on Sundays is a gift of God. How well are we using this
time in the service of God's purposes? When was our
programme for Sundays last reviewed, and on what
basis are decisions made about the programme? Could
we grow better by having, on occasion, a longer time of
fellowship on a Sunday? What about our ecumenical

resources? Taken as a whole, is the Sunday programme of the Christian organizations of your area either efficient or adventurous? What about other opportunities for good use of time?

4. We have buildings and equipment. Are we using them as a 'talent'? Are they things to use or things only to preserve? Is our stewardship at this point efficient and adventurous?

5. To whom is your church accountable? When, as a church, do you feel you are being required to give an account of your stewardship?

Finally, as a group, you could set yourself the task of working out a method by which the talents of members can be offered and celebrated in an act of worship, perhaps in an extended form of the offertory at the Eucharist.

18

Access for All

The Gospel Story

Matthew 21:1–17

Narrator	As Jesus and his disciples approached Jerusalem, they came to Bethphage at the Mount of Olives. There Jesus sent two of the disciples on ahead with these instructions:
Jesus	Go to the village there ahead of you, and at once you will find a donkey tied up with her colt beside her. Untie them and bring them to me. And if anyone says anything, tell him, 'The Master needs them'; and then he will let them go at once.
Narrator	This happened in order to make what the prophet had said come true:
Zechariah	Tell the city of Zion, Look, your king is coming to you! He is humble and rides on a donkey and a colt, the foal of a donkey.
Narrator	So the disciples went and did what Jesus had told them to do: they brought the donkey and the colt, threw their cloaks over them, and Jesus got on. A large

crowd of people spread their cloaks on the road while others cut branches from the trees and spread them on the road. The crowds walking in front of Jesus and those walking behind began to shout:

Leader of Crowd	Hosanna to the Son of David!
Crowd Chorus	God bless him who comes in the name of the Lord! Hosanna in the highest!
Narrator	When Jesus entered Jerusalem, the whole city was thrown into an uproar, saying:
Leader of Citizens	Who is this?
Citizens' Chorus	Who is this?
Narrator	The crowds said:
Leader of Crowd	This is the prophet.
Crowd Chorus	This is the prophet Jesus, from Nazareth in Galilee.
Narrator	Jesus went into the Temple and drove out all those who were buying and selling there. He overturned the tables of the money-changers and the stools of those who sold pigeons and said to them:
Jesus	It is written in the Scriptures that God said, 'My Temple will be called a house of prayer.' But you are making it a hideout for thieves!
Narrator	The blind and the crippled came to him in the Temple, and he healed them. The chief priests and the teachers of the Law became angry when they saw the wonderful things he was doing and the children shouting in the Temple:
Children	Hosanna to the Son of David!

Narrator	So they asked Jesus:
Chief priest	Do you hear what they are saying?
Jesus	Indeed I do. Haven't you ever read this scripture? 'You have trained children and babies to offer perfect praise.'
Narrator	Jesus left them and went out of the city to Bethany, where he spent the night.

Making Connections

In Matthew's way of thinking, 'entering the Kingdom of Heaven', 'eternal life' and 'being saved' are different ways of saying the same thing. They are all about entering the new age that Jesus is bringing.

This is another story about a journey. Jesus comes to the city of Jerusalem as the new ruler, the new government of God. He comes claiming access, first for himself, and then for those for whom access has been denied.

This is an ancient theme, celebrated many times in the psalms. We can see the pattern very clearly in Psalm 24. I give here a version of this old song in a way that expresses its character as a celebratory dialogue. It is a song of pilgrimage. There are two main groups of people: the pilgrims who are approaching the city, and the citizens whose home the city is. I give it here with a repeated chorus, along the lines of a traditional antiphon.[1]

Chorus (pilgrims)	**Let the Lord enter:**
Chorus (citizens)	**He is the King of Glory.**
Leader (citizens)	The earth is the Lord's and its fullness, The world and all its peoples. It is he that set it on the seas; On the waters he made it firm.
Chorus (pilgrims)	**Let the Lord enter:**
Chorus (citizens)	**He is the King of Glory.**

Leader (pilgrims)	Who shall climb the mountain of the Lord? Who shall stand in his holy place?
Leader (citizens)	Those with clean hands and pure heart, Who trust not in fraud and deception.
Chorus (pilgrims)	**Let the Lord enter:**
Chorus (citizens)	**He is the King of Glory.**
Leader (citizens)	They shall receive blessings from the Lord, And reward from the God who saves us.
Leader (pilgrims)	Such are the folk who seek him, Seek the face of the God of Jacob.
Chorus (pilgrims)	**Let the Lord enter:**
Chorus (citizens)	**He is the King of Glory.**
Leader (pilgrims)	O Gates, lift high your heads; Grow higher, ancient doors; Let him enter, the King of Glory; Let him enter, the King of Glory.
Chorus (pilgrims)	**Let the Lord enter:**
Chorus (citizens)	**He is the King of Glory.**
Leader (citizens)	Who is the King of Glory?
Leader (pilgrims)	The Lord, the mighty, the valiant, The Lord, the valiant in the struggle; He is the King of Glory.
Chorus (pilgrims):	**Let the Lord enter:**
Chorus (citizens):	**He is the King of Glory.**
Leader (citizens)	Who is the King of Glory? Who is the King of Glory?
Leader (pilgrims)	He, the Lord of all powers; He is the King of Glory.
Chorus (pilgrims):	**Let the Lord enter:**
Chorus (citizens):	**He is the King of Glory.**
Leaders together	Give glory to the Father Almighty,

To his Son, Jesus Christ our Lord,
To the Spirit who dwells in our hearts
Both now and for ever, Amen.

Chorus (pilgrims)　　**Let the Lord enter:**
Chorus (citizens)　　**He is the King of Glory.**

The Psalm starts with the boldest statement in the Bible, that the whole creation is God's property. That is what the City of God stands for. That is what the Temple celebrates. This is God's world. God made it according to his own design, to include all in his purpose of order and justice. It is not a whole lot of commodities, to be fought over and split up among groups who claim ownership or domination for themselves. It is one good creation. This is the statement to which the responsible citizens are committed, which they repeat to themselves and to the world. They are at home on the mountain of God's City. They are at home with this belief; they cherish it; it gives them their meaning.

Then there is a group of people who are on the way up. They are not there yet. So they enquire, 'What are the qualifications for belonging in your community? Can we climb up and join you?' They get a traditional answer: 'You can come in, if you are honest, if you avoid defrauding other people, if you are prepared to accept God's standards of justice and God's priorities and values.'

So far, a good clear affirmation of the traditional witness of the People of God. But then the pilgrims turn the dialogue around. Instead of merely seeking admission to the Lord's City for themselves, they claim that the great King of Glory is not safely inside the city with the citizens and priests, but is with the pilgrims outside, demanding access. The citizens have erected structures to keep other people out and to keep themselves secure. Whether they have intended to or not, they have made God an outsider. God is calling for these gates to be raised, so that he and his fellow-travellers can enter. The citizens admit their ignorance – or, perhaps, demand a password. Who is this King? The pilgrims have their answer clear and ready. The citizens seem to reply, 'We didn't quite catch that. Please repeat.' And the answer comes even more firmly, 'The Lord of hosts – your Lord and ours.'

(If you sing this psalm in the old Prayer Book version, you will miss the full significance of the dialogue. Even so, if you use the Anglican Chant composed by the old Victorian Sir Joseph Barnby, you will find that it fits the words extraordinarily well. The flow of the melody for 'Who is the King of Glory?' is exactly the intonation of the speech of a person asking such a question.)

God, in the psalm, is the King of power. He comes, claiming and demanding access. He is alongside of those who are seeking, who are on the way, who are trying to climb, who are not sure of their qualifications. God is pilgrim.

But, in another favourite picture in the imagination of God's people, God is more gentle and gracious. He is the bridegroom, coming to claim his bride. He is looking forward to having access to her. She will be ready for him; she will open herself for him, so that he can enter and be in her and belong in her. The Song of Songs is, primarily, a wonderful erotic poem, full of delight and tenderness. But the tradition is wise and gracious, which sees it as a song of the romance between God and his people. And, for Christians, the bridegroom is Christ.

Jesus comes to the city, fulfilling the psalm, but in a gentler mode: not as a powerful monarch erect on a war-horse, but as a pilgrim alongside the Galilean poor. He is mounted, certainly, but on a donkey; the eyes of a donkey-rider are no higher than those of the pedestrians around. He comes as a king who is on the level. He drives a one-donkey-power vehicle. The average speed of such a vehicle is rather lower than that of the average pedestrian. He comes claiming access; he is himself the accessible one.

Nearly 30 years ago, I was a member of a delegation that was urgently seeking to persuade the British government to take action to discourage a big multi-national mining company from exploiting the poor and disenfranchised people of Namibia. After a wait of several weeks, we were given a formal interview with a senior official of the Foreign and Commonwealth Office. We were taken down what seemed to be miles of corridors; we had a stilted conversation which felt like a tennis match, with the ball being knocked back and forth between the officials and ourselves. Every word was recorded by secretaries (a secretary being one who keeps secrets). A couple of days later, I was with a small group of university lecturers and students in Dublin, and I happened to mention this issue. One of the lecturers said, 'I'm sure our Government can do something about this. I'll be taking coffee with the Secretary to the Treasury tomorrow morning and I'll put it to him.' Access!

Jesus comes, claiming access. With him are the 'crowds'. These are the disenfranchised and landless peasants, people with no rights, people who are virtually exiles in their own land. They come with their song of 'Hosanna', which in Hebrew is a cry of appeal and acclamation, 'Save, we pray'. The crowds see in Jesus the one who brings salvation, who can give them access to the space and the citizenship that have been stolen from them. The secure cosmopolitan citizens of the capital city, who have all the advantages of communication, of education and of access to the centres of power and holiness, are forced to ask, 'Who is this?' They do not know. But those who have travelled, the pilgrims on the fringe, they know. Jesus is their home-boy. 'This is Jesus, the prophet from Galilee; we can tell you, he's come with us; like us, he's a provincial from the far north.'

Jesus, as Saviour, comes making space for those for whom there is no space.

He enters the city, and moves to the Temple. It is well known that, in the Temple, there were notices that warned

Gentiles of the terrible penalties that they would suffer if they dared to pass the barriers. The Temple was reserved for the Jews. But the Temple did have a feature that most Christian Churches do not have; it had an area set aside for people who were not qualified to enter the sanctuary. There was a space that recognized that Gentiles should have some access to the place of holiness. This was 'The Court of the Gentiles'. It was supposed to stand for the truth that God is God of all people and not only of the people of Israel. But this area had been taken over as a place of financial exchange. The area that should have given space to the outsider and the enquirer was cluttered up with the apparatus for ensuring the Temple's economic security. The space that had been set aside for those who were culturally disadvantaged had been invaded by the power of money and accumulation. Mark's version of the story stresses this, by quoting Jesus as recalling that the Temple was supposed to be a 'house of prayer for all nations'.

The Temple, under the authority of Rome, was able to operate its own currency, made out of especially pure silver from Tyre. The Temple tax had to be paid with these coins, and all transactions for purchase of animals and birds for sacrifice had to be conducted in this currency. The bureaux de change that provided this currency were able to set their own charges for exchanges; and the Temple authorities, the priests, got their share of the profits. To be a Temple priest was to have a comfortable and secure lifestyle. As they saw it, their job required them to insist on a strict adherence to the rules of purity; their demand for high standards inevitably meant high prices to be paid by the poor, high profits for those who controlled the equipment for the pursuit of holiness. Religion can be an expensive business.

All this stirs Jesus to commit the most violent of his recorded activities. He doesn't ask for any permission. He doesn't use any diplomacy. He causes complete chaos. He wrecks the timetable and procedures of the sacrificial structure. He exposes the impurity at the heart of a system that prides itself on its commitment to national purity. He causes major civic disturbance. This is an outrageous thing to do. Although no one is killed or physically injured, as an attack on the most precious symbol of the national identity, this would feel as shocking as the attack on the twin towers of the World Trade Center on 11 September 2001. And it is all for the sake of making space for people who were being denied access, either through being too poor, or too sinful, or through being of the wrong race.

People with disabilities would find it hard to know how to think of themselves, in the times of the Bible – as they still do. On the one hand, there are places where the Law of God seeks to protect them and to assert their rights. It curses, for instance, those who put a stumbling-block in the way of the blind – and it is difficult to see why anyone would do this except as a perverted practical joke. But it also sees disability as a sign that creation has gone wrong; a disabled person is an insult to the Creator, and therefore ought not to be allowed to compromise the purity of the sanctuary. The blind and the lame were an offence to King David, who created Jerusalem as the pre-eminent place of God's abiding; so there was to be no place for them in the Temple (2 Samuel 5:6–8). Jesus, who is being acknowledged here as Son of David, takes an exactly opposite view. He sees some disabled people, who have managed to enter where they had no right to be. He makes no objection to their defiance; he makes himself accessible to them, and heals them. David's attitude, and the tradition that followed his example, could only protect the non-disabled from contamination; Jesus gives access, and the disabled are in first.

'Children's voices in the sanctuary! Children spoiling the peace and quiet of the holy place! That will never do!' This is altogether too much for the religious leadership, and they protest. Jesus replies that God perfects his praise in the cries of those who have least power and status. The accessible king affirms the right of children to be there – and to lead the worship. The old must learn from the young; the young recognize the Messiah, and he makes space for them. Education, seniority and maturity are not required as qualifications for access to Jesus.

The keepers of the Temple believe that it is their job to preserve the place of holiness from pollution by unbelieving outsiders, disabled people, and children. In making access, Jesus is not merely being compassionate; he is not just allowing them in as afterthoughts. Without them, the fellowship of the Temple is incomplete. They belong.

Jesus' violent action is a protest against the forms of violence that cause most hurt to the weakest children of God. The power of unrestrained finance brings not only poverty but also exclusion, resentment and death. Jesus' action is a stinging reminder to the powers of religion that they must watch out for this violence and not be co-opted into it. It was by a deep instinctive perception of these connections that the sculptor Eric Gill was inspired, in 1923, to choose this theme of Christ driving the money-changers out of the Temple as the subject of his War Memorial at Leeds University. Not discouraged by the furious controversy that this aroused, he went on to propose the same theme for a massive sculpture for the new League of Nations building in Geneva.[2]

Jesus is acting in complete confidence in his own authority. But he is not merely behaving as a maverick, flouting convention for the sake of flouting convention. The authorities would no doubt call him a loose cannon. But at every point he is claiming the authority of the deepest traditions of the Scripture. He is out of step with contemporary custom, because contemporary custom has deserted God's purposes. He is moving against the times, because the times are moving in the wrong direction. He is not conservative in the modern political sense – that is so often merely a project for protecting the interests of those who have been doing well out of the social processes of the last generation or two. But, in a deeper sense, Jesus, like many prophets, is fundamentally conservative. He is standing for values that his contemporaries have abandoned. He is claiming space for those whose interests have been the special concern of the Law of God. So Matthew is careful to point out that, in these actions, Jesus is doing things that fulfil the purpose of God, as disclosed in the word of God handed down from the past.

Through Jesus, we have access to the Father. That is Paul's summary of the effect of the work of Jesus. Jesus makes the holy one accessible. That is what the Temple was supposed to do. Jesus is the new Temple. We Christians still have sanctuaries; and they are supposed to have the same purpose. Sometimes our sanctuaries are claimed as places of refuge by people who are on the wrong side of our systems of law and control – and, indeed, sometimes the places that are claimed in this way are places that, by their beauty of light and colour and symbol, do speak most clearly of the transcendence of God. This may well be close to the vision of sanctuary that Jesus affirms. The institution is judged according to the effect that it has for those who get least advantage from the status quo – the outsider, the disabled, the children. It was this kind of issue that inspired the conscience of Jesus, and drove him to costly, violent and controversial action. All of us have some responsibility for the formation of conscience, whether we are designated Church leaders or ministers, or teachers, or friends or sponsors of confirmation candidates – a very fruitful type of ministry, as I have observed it – or whatever. We should ask ourselves – and this is a very proper question for a church council or Synod – about what subjects have we been educating people, so that they feel them to be matters of conscience?

For Working Groups

Ignition

In my office as a Bishop, I had a cartoon that depicted a vicar's wife calling her husband and saying, 'There's someone outside saying he wants to speak to a minister but he doesn't like organized religion.' The vicar replies, from his desk, 'Show him straight in; he won't find any religion more disorganized than this one.' Matthew's story shows Jesus vigorously disorganizing a religious organization, and any realistic study of the story is likely to turn out to be a fairly disorganized experience. So be prepared for anything.

This is a story that benefits from being worked on by a fairly large group – anything between about 36 and 80. So it might work best with a whole congregation rather than a small study-group. It would also be best if used for an all-age event, since children have an important part.

Either
How much horse-power do you require to move yourself around? If you need more than, say, 100 horse-power, isn't that a sign that you must be either a very heavy person or a very weak person?

Or
Do you know of a town where you have to climb a steep hill in order to reach the traditional town-centre? Perhaps Harlech, or Bridgnorth, or Lincoln or Geneva? Such places are, in fact, not very common in Britain. But this is what Jerusalem is like. Jesus and his fellow-pilgrims might well be a bit out of breath by the time came for getting the donkey.

Exploration

Not a great deal of introduction will be needed. It could be useful to perform Psalm 24 in the way described, as a way of getting into the relationship between the pilgrims and the citizens. The pilgrims start from the farthest end of the space away from the citizens, and gradually move towards them.

Read the story of Matthew 21 from *The Dramatised Bible*, as supplied here. Recognize that it is about a journey. This can be emphasized either by sketching it out in a diagram on an overhead projector, or by arranging the furniture on the floor to represent the various stages that Jesus travels through.

Break into nine teams (if you have enough people for more teams, divide teams 3 and 5 into two):

1 Jesus
2 The disciples and pilgrims from Galilee/the crowd
3 The doctors of the Law and chief priests
4 The citizens of Jerusalem
5 The buyers and sellers, the bureaux de change officials, and the pigeon-dealers
6 The Gentiles
7 The disabled
8 The children
9 Matthew, our story-teller

Questions for Jesus: *What are your main motives and feelings? (See Luke 19:41–44.) What exactly are you trying to do? Why do you act as you do?*

Why use the donkey?
At the end of the day,
how do you feel about
what has happened?

Questions for the disciples,
pilgrims from Galilee/crowd:

What is happening to
you? What is the
effect of the day on
you? Who do you
sympathize with?

Questions for the
doctors of the Law,
the chief priests, the
Jerusalem citizens,
the buyers and sellers, the
bureaux de change officials,
and the pigeon-dealers:

What sort of people
are you? What are
your main interests
and motives? What
do you think about
Jesus? How does your
opinion about Jesus
change during the
day? (For the buyers
and sellers, see
Jeremiah 7:1–11; for
the bureaux de
change officials and
pigeon-dealers, see
Leviticus 1:14;
Luke 2:23–24.)

Questions for the Gentiles:

How do you feel about
the day's events? Do
they mean anything

Questions for the disabled:

Questions for the children:

Questions for Matthew:

to you? (See Mark 11:17; Isaiah 56:6–8.) What was it like to be disabled? What does the presence of Jesus mean to you? How do you feel about the day's events as a whole? (See Leviticus 19:14; 21:16–20; 2 Samuel 5:6–8.) What is happening to you? What do you feel about Jesus and the day's events? (See Matthew 18:1–6; Mark 10:13–16.) You are a member of the community that have become disciples of Jesus. Why do you think that this story is so worth telling? What use do you think it is going to be for your fellow-believers? Why do you tell it in the way you do?

If you do have an all-age group, don't put all the children together into the 'Children' team; instead, distribute them throughout the teams.

After a few minutes for the teams to get into the experience of their characters, the group leader can give people general freedom to move around and confront each other. The questions for everyone can be: *During the course of today's events, do you feel that you have got any new friends or enemies? Who have you come close to? Who do you want to confront? How do you want to express what has happened?*

You may want to enact the whole story, so let people find something to represent the donkey (a bicycle?), tables, birdcages, money-boxes (computers?) – anything. It may get quite violent, so take precautions for children who might be scared.

Once we had an evicted pigeon-seller (in fact, a huge African man with a massive voice), who immediately responded by starting up a new stall, getting a corner in the market for second-hand camels! On another occasion, a team of 'children' (who, as it happened, were mainly elderly) started up a kind of Hosanna conga-dance which caught up most of the other members; it trundled all around the meeting-place and upset practically everything. I also remember a team of 'children' who were all university students; they refused to play, and spent their time in a learned analysis of the sociopolitical structures implicit in the story. There's room for everyone! The confusion and disturbance is all part of what the story is about, so don't try too hard to avoid it.

After the experience has gone on long enough, the group leader can try to call everyone to order.

Destination

How accessible is your church to disabled people, children or 'outsiders'? How far do the interests of those who 'belong' get in the way of those who don't?

What would you do if someone claimed 'sanctuary' in your church?

How are the powers of money-wealth invading the space that should be kept for the poor and for God? Who is able to say 'Take this away from here'?

Check the final question in the main exposition section of this chapter, above. This will probably be quite enough to think about, without any other formal questions.

19

He Cannot Save Himself

The Gospel Story

Mark 15:27–39

Narrator	They also crucified two bandits with Jesus, one on his right and the other on his left. People passing by shook their heads and hurled insults at Jesus:
Persons 1 and 2	Aha!
Person 1	You were going to tear down the Temple and build it up again in three days!
Person 2	Now come down from the cross and save yourself!
Narrator	In the same way the chief priests and the teachers of the Law jeered at Jesus, saying to each other:
Lawyer 1	He saved others, but he cannot save himself!
Lawyer 2	Let us see the Messiah, the king of Israel, come down from the cross now, and we will believe in him!
Narrator	And the two who were crucified with Jesus insulted him also. At noon the whole country was covered with darkness, which lasted for three hours. At three o'clock Jesus cried out with a loud shout:

Jesus	Eloi, Eloi, lema sabachthani?
Narrator	Which means: My God, my God, why did you abandon me? Some of the people there heard him and said:
Person 1	Listen, he is calling for Elijah!
Narrator	One of them ran up with a sponge, soaked it in cheap wine, and put it on the end of a stick. Then he held it up to Jesus' lips and said:
Person 2	Wait! Let us see if Elijah is coming to bring him down from the cross!
Narrator	With a loud cry Jesus died.
	The curtain hanging in the Temple was torn in two, from top to bottom. The army officer who was standing there in front of the cross saw how Jesus had died. He said:
Officer	This man was really the Son of God!

Making Connections

Earlier in the story, Jesus has been saving other people. He is with the Disciples when they are almost lost at sea; he is with them in the boat – but gives the impression that he is not there at all. They have to wake him. They call to him, 'Save, we are perishing'. He acts as saviour (Matthew 8:25). But they have needed his salvation only because they have followed him. We can imagine Peter's wife's reaction: 'You should have stayed at home in bed, instead of going off after that crazy preacher; then you wouldn't have got into that mess!'

Christ is reliably present with his friends, even when he seems not to be. He is God with us, Emmanuel.

On 11 September 2001, the people on those hijacked aircraft must have been praying, 'Save, Lord, we are perishing.' And they did perish. The hijackers were confident of a certain type of salvation; and they achieved it. They left some evidence of their triumphant idea of God.[1] We can understand, to some extent, how people could see what they did and think privately to themselves, 'What a wonderful way to die' – better even than Samson, the biblical model for a mass-murderer who dies by suicide, using the technology supplied by his victims (Judges 16:30). But that is very different from the way that Christ dies. He dies in confusion and disgrace. It is people who die like that who can feel the companionship of Christ.

So we hear the cynical comment of the lawyers, in the story of the crucifixion of Jesus. This is the last time that the word 'save' occurs in Mark's Gospel. What Jesus does for other people he does not do for himself. He creates space for others; he allows himself to be confined on the pole of the cross. He gives sight to the blind, but he allows himself to be deprived of sight by the blindfolding. He ministers to the deaf, but he allows the most precious faculty for deaf people, his vision, to be removed; and he behaves like a deaf man in the presence of his accusers. He delivers others from the restrictiveness of the purity regulations; but he allows those regulations to have their vengeance on him.

One of the truest paintings of the Crucifixion is the central panel of the Isenheim Altarpiece by Matthias Grünewald (c. 1515). It was not conceived as a piece of romantic self-expression by the artist, but as a technical instrument of therapy in a hospital for lepers and victims of bubonic plague. Grünewald depicts Christ with his flesh all over pock-marks. Literally, these are, of course, from the scourging. But they will enable the leper and the plague-patient to see 'the Son of God has skin which is as afflicted as my own'. The huge finger of John the Baptist points at the Crucified Christ: look at that – that is what salvation means for you. Elsewhere in the altarpiece, one of the great symbols of power is feathers. The skin of the Crucified is like that of a plucked fowl. He who brings the Kingdom has had all power drained from him.

To be true to the shape of the Gospel, this chapter of this book should balance out all the others. It is the other half of the story. Thus far, we have had stories of success. 'Salvation' has meant that the agent of God has been intervening to bring about change and renewal, to take part in the agenda of the people, especially the people who get little advantage from the systems of the world. Now we have salvation as failure, betrayal, loss of status, and death. The story of the arrest, trials and death of Jesus occupy about one-third of the text of the Gospels; it takes an even bigger proportion of the energies of Paul and of subsequent makers of theologies and creeds and liturgies.

'Himself he cannot save' is not such an unusual comment. Jesus himself expected his congregation at the synagogue at Nazareth to use the proverb, 'Doctor, heal yourself' against him (Luke 4:23). It is a common proverb, not only in Judaism.

The lawyers are wrong. The truth is not that he *cannot* save himself, but that he *chooses* not to save himself. At all sorts of levels, Jesus could have avoided his fate; he could have lived a long and useful life, and could have done pastoral work of great value to thousands of people. But, in the process of his arrest, trials, conviction and execution, he is the one person on the scene who did not make his own survival a priority. He dies; Caiaphas, Pilate, Barabbas, Peter, and the rest of them live to sleep another night and to work another day.

Again, this is not unique. One unit of the New York Fire Department lost every one of its members on 11 September 2001. In principle, this was a predictable result of the occupation that they had decided to follow, to die on behalf of the community.

What is unusual in the Christ-story is the understanding of the place of God. Most theologies expect that God will be the bringer of success, of victory, of dominance. God will be on the side of the winner. The winner will be evidence of the validity of God. The institutions that celebrate this God will see themselves as being in business to congratulate the powerful on being powerful. Such is the role of God, right across human cultures. The Christian tradition in Britain is not immune from this motive. But one community arose which learned a different song. Long before Jesus, Judaism had an insight into a God who would be on the side of the loser. In his ministry, Jesus was God on the side of the losers. In his dying, Jesus was God the loser himself. Consequently, as Mark's story shows only too clearly, God seems to be useless in a crisis.

God does not fit neatly into our agenda. He is not just there at our convenience. Even if we have got the attention of Jesus, as Jairus did, we may find that our programme with him is interrupted. And that story may give some clues about the reasons for God's delays. We sometimes speak of Jesus as the man who was always available for others. Not really true. Early in his ministry, his friends told him that everyone was looking for him, wanting his attention; 'So, let's go somewhere else,' he replies (Mark 1:38).

The twentieth-century German martyr, Dietrich Bonhoeffer, imprisoned and awaiting execution on account of his resistance to the Nazis, knew something of this.

The God who is with us is the God who forsakes us . . . God allows himself to be edged out of the world and onto the cross . . . It is not by his omnipotence that Christ helps us, but by his weakness and suffering . . . Man's religiosity makes him look in his distress to the power of God in the world. The Bible however directs him to the powerlessness and suffering of God; only a suffering God can help.

Men go to God when they are sore bestead,
Pray to him for succour, for his peace, for bread,
For mercy for them sick, sinning, or dead:
All men do so, Christian and unbelieving.

Men go to God when he is sore bestead,
Find him poor and scorned, without shelter or bread,
Whelmed under weight of the wicked, the weak, the dead:
Christians stand by God in his hour of grieving.

God goeth to every man when sore bestead,
Feedeth body and spirit with his bread,
For Christians, heathens alike he hangeth dead:
And both alike forgiving.[2]

We could leave the matter there, as J.S. Bach leaves us at the end of his great accounts of the Passion according to Matthew and John. And that would be good. This is not a matter for elaborate exercises. But it should still claim our imagination and our attempts at empathy. We are supposed to be doing theology; and the final test of theology is how far it enables us to love God. That is no simple or sentimental test; but it is a test that goes beyond our ability to put things into words or to organize projects.

But we do need to go a bit further. If this chapter is, properly, the other half of the whole book, how do the two halves fit together? They fit together because the active Christ and the suffering Christ are both alive now with us, inviting us to continue the process. They fit together because of the resurrection of Jesus. But the resurrection is not a magical device to tell us that everything was all right after all. It wasn't. The powers of darkness came out in full force to destroy the Son of God. The combined efforts of the best law in the world, the best religion in the world, and the unanimous vote of the general public brought about the judicial murder of God. God is the loser. But God remains God.

The gospel is all about how to find and recognize God in his world. Conventional religion will tell us to look for God in the places of tranquillity and spiritual achievement, in situations like the 'Sabbath rest by Galilee' and the 'calm of hills above'. But Christ is God being known and met in the places of darkness and failure. God is met at the Cross. But this is not a sudden change of direction. As we have seen, Jesus' works of salvation were continually happening amid controversy and blame. Over 50 years ago, Canon (later Bishop) Joe Fison suggested some of the implications of this, in terms that now seem to have been amazingly prophetic.

If the cross is the clue to Christian faith, and the place where the secret of the blessing of the Father is found, then it will not be so much in the stability of an ordered society as in the anarchy of the breakdown of all law and order that we shall discover its secret today . . . Perhaps in the seething turmoil of the clashing ideologies of the iron curtain or in the desperate fanaticisms of the Middle East or in the terrible convulsions and mass pogroms and refugee migrations of the Punjab and the Far East, perhaps in the race discrimination of South Africa and the USA, perhaps in these places more than amongst the relics of a Victorian political and economic stability . . . this blessing may be found. The sentimental singing of Whittier's hymn and the preference for a faith valid in the beauty and isolation of a Galilean hillside rather than in the dust and exploitation and mob fanaticism of Jerusalem is hardly a faithful following of him, whose crowded Galilee of two thousand years ago had little in common with the loneliness of our Galilee today, but whose crowded and bigoted Jerusalem was so like our own. For him – and for us – the place of peace is the storm centre, not the circumference.[3]

I have to acknowledge that this insight of Joe Fison was one of the voices which made me take seriously the possibility that I might be called to serve in the increasingly grim situation of the apartheid regime in South Africa.

We have been looking at a whole series of incidental characters in the story of Jesus: a paralysed man and his friends; a woman of dubious reputation and abundant hair; a little business man with a bad image; sundry lepers; a scared woman who has had a bad experience of the medical profession; a puzzled lawyer; a pagan non-commissioned officer; a defiant mother; and so on. They come onto the stage, have a short spell of fame, and then are heard of no more. It's a succession of miscellaneous encounters, each of them of intrinsic interest, but with no great coherence; a succession of dropped stitches, of items clicked into the recycle bin. If we had set out to make a planned strategy of action, susceptible to proper review and evaluation, surely we would have made a better job of it than this. What links them together is the figure of Christ. These are no longer just miscellaneous events from long ago and far away. We see them as threads that are knit together to make a fabric of salvation for us now. The stitches are picked up, items returned to the screen, a scattered program defragmented, in the process of the gospel. They make sense for us, not as old stories but as models of how God in action is to be recognized. But without the resurrection of Jesus, these characters would never be known to us. Or, if by some chance their stories were recorded, this would be merely in the same kind of way as we might hear of anecdotes about Roman emperors, of antiquarian interest, perhaps, but of no cutting-edge for us today.

Do we find that these stories have more than mere

antiquarian interest? Do they in fact work for us? Do they in fact enable us to recognize God's activity in the world, and to work with that activity? Do they enable us to go on being the Body of Christ, saying the Christ word, experiencing the Christ experience, acting the Christ act, suffering the Christ suffering? If, in any small way, we can say 'Yes', then this is due to the fact that they are stories of the living Christ; and all these characters are resurrected with Christ, so that we discover them here and now as colleagues in our world. He takes the bread, and breaks it, and tells us that this breaking is what is happening to his body. But he does not ask us to be merely spectators. He says, 'Do this yourselves; let what has been happening to me happen to you'.

The bread is broken 'in the same night when he was betrayed' (I think that it is a real loss when this traditional phrase is dropped from the Eucharistic Prayer). Every Eucharist happens in a betraying world and is done by a betraying church and a betraying priest. The priest who has the awesome duty of saying these words is also an agent of Christ's mandate to absolve the sinner in Confession; she or he knows better than most people the extent and effectiveness of the conspiracy of betrayal in which we humans have become trapped. But this is itself part of the gospel of salvation. The failures and forgiven-ness of us disciples have become part of the continuing Gospel. The small successes of little people are knit into the fabric of salvation. This is because Christ continues to be the risen one, who defeats the erosion and wastage of time. In Christ, our struggle is not lost. There is no wastage.

In the year 2000, the Irish poet and Nobel prize-winner, Seamus Heaney, came to speak to the Wilfred Owen Association in Shrewsbury. Towards the end of the meeting, someone asked him whether he was optimistic about the future, particularly with reference to Ireland. He made a helpful distinction: 'Optimism says, "We are going to win." Hope says, "What we are doing is worth doing." I have hope.'

St Paul makes a great exposition of the truth of resurrection in 1 Corinthians 15; after a long build-up of wonderful image and metaphor, celebrating the great hope of the new thing breaking into the old, he ends up quite simply, saying, that it is all worth doing: '*Therefore*, my beloved, be steadfast, immovable, always excelling in the work of the Lord, because you know that in the Lord your labour is not in vain.'

For Working Groups

Although this is very different from the previous chapters, it would be a pity if the working group failed to address this story. The programme need not follow the same pattern as the other chapters; but the members can share with each other their responses to such questions as these:

- What strikes us as especially interesting in this story?
- Where are we in the story?
- Who has experience of failure, loss, helplessness, the absence of God, the uselessness of God in a crisis?
- Who has seen the truth about God in a situation where God seems to be denied?
- Who has seen an 'outsider', like the centurion, recognizing a truth which, for the 'insiders', the lawyers, is just absurd?
- Who has seen how some sort of coherence can begin to make sense of things that appear to be random and pointless?

- What are we praying for when we pray for the Middle East, or Afghanistan, or Southern Africa?

Perhaps you can see this sort of process at work, in the Church, in the world around you, or in your own life. There is a mystery of hope that makes hopeless situations seem to be worthwhile – the Seamus Heaney insight.

There may be new ways in which you can work with God, especially in taking the side of those for whom there is no obvious cure.

This may all be quite testing. Try to avoid easy platitudes, but sometimes a remark that seems to be mere conventional piety may be a person's way of expressing something very deep and true for them. But be willing to wait, to be silent, to listen doubly carefully to each other's hesitant vision or expectant pain. Be willing to take other people into your darkness. Be willing to be taken by other people into their darkness. And the risen Christ will be there.

A final word with the Evangelist

We come to the last of our extracts from an interview which might have been given by the Evangelist Mark to Dudley, a local theologian.

Dudley That last big story of yours, the story of the arrest and trial and crucifixion of Jesus: we all treasure this; it is the story which we all go back to. Thank you for putting it so clearly and starkly. This is indeed a Son of God that we can

	believe in. But I'm afraid we have all sorts of problems with the section you put in just before.[4]
Mark	Like what?
Dudley	It all seems so obscure. All this about earthquakes, tribulations, stars falling from heaven, fig trees, abomination of desolation. Some of our members are worried about such obscure things being reckoned as part of the Gospel. Some of us think that it's all about the Last Day. Are we right?
Mark.	Funny that you should have problems with that lot. That was the part that we all found easiest – easiest to understand, I mean, not easiest to cope with.
Dudley	The abomination of desolation?
Mark	Aye, well, don't you see, I did say 'Let the reader make sense of this'. With the security-police breathing down your necks you've got to use a bit of code. Our people knew exactly what it was about. It was happening all around them. Our people were being handed over to the system, every other day. We knew all about this handing over, this betraying; look how often I pointed it out – here, and here, and here. And here, in the story of Jesus, a bit later on, handed over, handed over, handed over. You say that you value the story of Jesus. But what do you mean? Is it happening for you? Because that's why it was important

for us. It made sense of the crisis that we ourselves were in. So, when I wrote that section that you have problems with, I wrote it because it showed how the story of Jesus was coming up to date for us.

Dudley   So, it's not really about the Last Day at all?

Mark   Yes, well, it's as if the Last Day is as close as last night. It's all happening. Like Jesus brought the next world next door. It's all happening – isn't it – isn't it? Or aren't you close enough to the action in Telford? Can you see it for yourself?

Dudley   I'm not sure. I'm not sure that we have sufficient information to be able to know where everything fits in.

Mark   Watch out, my friend, you're not expected to *know*. Some of you thesis-bashers are far too keen on knowing everything, yes, and controlling everything into the bargain. That's just not an option for most of the little people who try to love God. Look, even Jesus didn't know.[5] You're expected to watch, to be ready to recognize. We have given you enough idea of what happens when God is present in his world. Go and see the signs around you. Go and belong in the story yourself.

Blessed John Mark Evangelist, pray for us.

Notes and References

Chapters 3–8 and 13 are substantially developed from material in John D. Davies and John J. Vincent, *Mark at Work*, London: Bible Reading Fellowship, 1980, used here by courtesy of Dr Vincent and the publishers. Chapters 15 and 17 are substantially developed from material in John D. Davies, *World on Loan*, London: Bible Society, 1993, used here by courtesy of the publishers.

1 Jesus the Story-Maker

1 Eric James, *In Season, out of Season*, London: SCM Press, 1999, p. 186.
2 This pioneering parish and its policies are described in E.W. Southcott, *The Parish Comes Alive*, Oxford: Mowbray, 1956.
3 For the use of 'save' and 'salvation' in the Infancy stories in Matthew and Luke, see John Davies, *Be Born in Us Today*, Norwich: Canterbury Press, 1999, pp. 106, 124ff.
4 See the report *Partners in Life: The Handicapped and the Church*, Geneva: World Council of Churches, 1979, especially the essays by Lesslie Newbigin and Ulrich Bach, pp. 17–53. See also Roy McCoughry and Wayne Morris, *Making a World of Difference*, London: SPCK, 2002, a book which goes creatively far beyond my attempts here to reflect on what is called 'disability'.

2 Meanings of 'Salvation'

1 Quoted in Edward Robinson, *The Language of Mystery*, London: SCM Press, 1987, p. 38.
2 Quoted in Ned Thomas, *The Welsh Extremist*, London: Victor Gollancz, 1971, p. 125.
3 *The Mystery of Salvation*, London: Church House Publishing, 1995.

4 A Method for Working with a Story

1 Laurie Green, *Let's Do Theology*, London: Mowbray, 1990, p. 26.

2 Ian Fraser, *Re-inventing Theology as the People's Work*, Glasgow: Wild Goose Publications, 1980, pp. 68ff.

3 Green, *Let's Do Theology*, pp. 26ff. and *passim*.

4 Two writers who combine creative imagination and disciplined attention to the text are Gerd Theissen (*The Shadow of the Galilean*, London: SCM Press, 1987) and Dorothy L. Sayers (*The Man Born to be King*, London: Victor Gollancz, 1943). Sayers demonstrates how the professional skills of a dramatist can contribute to a scholarly understanding of the Gospel text – and this in a series of radio plays for children!

5 Getting Started

1 See John D. Davies, *The Faith Abroad*, Oxford: Basil Blackwell, 1983, p. 69. See also Kenneth Leech, *The Eye of the Storm*, London: Darton, Longman & Todd, 1992, pp. 179–83, on the figure of Saul Alinsky.

2 C.G. Jung, *The Integration of the Personality*, London: Kegan Paul, 1940, p. 295.

3 D. Bonhoeffer, *Life Together*, London: SCM Press, 1954, p. 67.

4 The Greek of Mark's Gospel is a pretty rough manger for the cradling of the newly expressed word of God. It is not as fluent or as competent as the Greek of writers such as Luke and Paul. One of Mark's favourite words, which he uses about 40 times, is one that can be translated as 'immediately' or 'at once' or 'straightaway'. So, while Mark is a sensitive man (he, more than most of the Evangelists, tells us about Jesus' feelings), he seems to be a down-to-earth character who likes to get on with the story.

5 How often do you see Mark 16:1–8 specified as the main Sunday Gospel reading, and not just as an alternative?

6 Going through the Roof

1 F.W. Robertson, *Sermons Preached at Brighton: Third Series*, London: Kegan Paul, Trench, Trubner, 1897, pp. 70ff. See also John Davies, *Affirming Confession*, London: Darton, Longman & Todd, 1995.

9 *The Foreign Soldier's Prayer: 'Only Say the Word'*

1 Jeffrey John, *The Meaning in the Miracles*, Norwich: Canterbury Press, 2001, p. 159. This is a valuable source of insights into the miracle-stories of the Gospels, and I am grateful for the opportunity to have seen it at an early stage of its production.

2 Sayers, *The Man Born to be King*, pp. 130ff.

3 Mark 15:21; 14:51–52.

4 There are many places in the Bible that indicate the revulsion that a Jewish man like John Mark would feel about uncircumcised men, e.g. 1 Samuel 17:26; Ezekiel 32:20–30; Acts 11:3. We cannot be sure that Mark 14:51–52 is actually about him personally; but even if it is not, he would surely share these common feelings. Paul's revolutionary insight must have seemed thoroughly disgusting to many of his kinsmen (Galatians 5:6; 6:15; 1 Corinthians 7:19). The English word 'circumcised' exactly corresponds to the Greek word – literally, 'cut round'; but the Greek word translated 'uncircumcised' is quite different, and literally means 'foreskin', a thoroughly insulting word in Jewish vocabulary. To be on display, totally naked, was one of the most scandalous aspects of crucifixion, a deliberate piece of cultural cruelty. There is no historical justification for the loincloths with which artists have traditionally eased the offence. In the incident of the sheet that night, Mark was personally sharing, in a small way, the disgrace experienced by the Saviour – good reason for him to mention it; good reason, perhaps, for the other Evangelists to leave it out.

10 *The Prayer of Defiant Access*

1 Theissen, *The Shadow of the Galilean*, p. 191.

12 *Bending the Mind of the Lawyer*

1 Oscar Wilde, *De Profundis* (in *The Works of Oscar Wilde*, London: Collins, 1992, p. 878).

13 *The Opening Programme*

1 See Doug Alker, *Really Not Interested in the Deaf?*, Darwen: D. Alker, 2000.

14 The Ten Per Cent Return

1 Waldo Williams, quoted in A.M. Allchin, *Praise Above All*, Cardiff: University of Wales Press, 1991, p. 3.

15 The Public Climb-Down

1 Wilde, *De Profundis*, p. 874.
2 Jim Wallis, *The Call to Conversion*, New York: Harper & Row, 1982, p. 46.

16 The Blind who Sees

1 See John Hull, *In the Beginning There was Darkness*, London: SCM Press, 2001.
2 Hull, *In the Beginning*, p. 35.

17 Talent-Spotting

1 The 'Significance' of the scoring for the exercise 'Acknowledging Some of your Gifts' is as follows: each horizontal row represents one of the following activities, and your score reflects your potential interest and giftedness for it.

Row A is about Evangelizing.
Row B is about Teaching.
Row C is about Encouraging.
Row D is about Giving.
Row E is about Administering.
Row F is about Helping and Caring.

18 Access for All

1 Adapted from a version of Psalm 24 in *The Psalms, a New Translation*, London: Collins, 1966, p. 49. This version provides a clear rhythm to the words. Each line of the 'Leaders' has three accents. The line for the chorus of pilgrims has a staccato rhythm, which the pilgrims can emphasize by 'knocking on the door' with their fists, on any convenient surface. The line for the chorus of citizens has three smoother beats, which can be emphasized by a hand-clap. To get the full effect of the text, the pilgrims should be

stationed at a distance from the citizens and gradually move towards them. A psalm is, of course, designed for singing and we have a simple chant to go with this version, which anyone interested can have for the asking.

2 Fiona MacCarthy, *Eric Gill*, London: Faber & Faber, 1989, pp. 166ff.

19 He Cannot Save Himself

1 See Rowan Williams, *Writing in the Dust: Reflections on 11th September and its Aftermath*, London: Hodder & Stoughton, 2002.

2 D. Bonhoeffer, *Letters and Papers from Prison*, London: SCM Press, 1953, p. 167.

3 J.E. Fison, *The Blessing of the Holy Spirit*, London: Longmans, Green, 1950, pp. 185–86, a deep and undervalued study of the doctrine of the Holy Spirit. Fison's books were both scholarly and practical, which I suppose accounts for the lack of attention given to them by both scholars and practitioners. He was a committed Evangelical, and appealed to me, as a young Anglo-Catholic, because he was at least as critical of the Evangelicals as he was of our lot.

4 Mark 13.

5 Mark 13.32–37.